Montañas de Anaga

Playa de las Teresitas

Iglesia de San Francisco,
Mercado Nuestra Señora de Africa,
Museo de la Naturaleza y el Hombre,
Museo Municipal de Bellas Artes,
Nuestra Señora de la Concepción,
Parque Municipal García Sanabria,
Plaza de la Candelaria & Plaza de España
Santa Cruz

*Parque Marítimo
César Manrique*

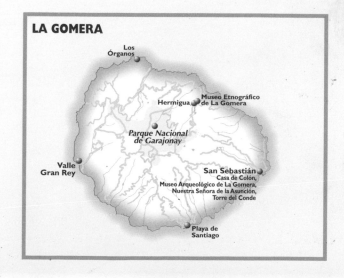

LA GOMERA

Los
Órganos

**Museo Etnográfico
de La Gomera**

Hermigua

*Parque Nacional
de Garajonay*

**Valle
Gran Rey**

San Sebastián
Casa de Colón,
Museo Arqueológico de La Gomera,
Nuestra Señora de la Asunción,
Torre del Conde

**Playa de
Santiago**

Scottish Borders

3 4144 0083 8966 6

TV
TENERIFE

BARBARA RADCLIFFE ROGERS AND STILLMAN ROGERS

If you have any comments
or suggestions for this guide
you can contact the editor at
Twinpacks@theAA.com

AA Publishing
Find out more about AA Publishing and the wide
range of services the AA provides by visiting our
website at theAA.com/bookshop

How to Use This Book

KEY TO SYMBOLS

✚ Map reference	▷ Further information
✉ Address	ℹ Tourist information
☎ Telephone number	✋ Admission charges: Expensive (over €9), Moderate (€3–€9), and Inexpensive (under €3)
🕐 Opening/closing times	
🍽 Restaurant or café	★ Major sight ★ Minor sight
🚌 Nearest bus route	👣 Walks 🚌 Drives
⛴ Nearest ferry route	
♿ Facilities for visitors with disabilities	🎁 Shops
	🎭 Entertainment and Activities
❓ Other practical information	🍴 Restaurants

This guide is divided into four sections

• **Essential Tenerife:** An introduction to the island and tips on making the most of your stay.
• **Tenerife by Area:** We've broken the island into three areas, plus one chapter for neighbouring La Gomera, and recommended the best sights, shops, activities, restaurants, entertainment and nightlife venues in each one. Suggested walks and drives help you to explore.
• **Where to Stay:** The best hotels, whether you're looking for luxury, budget or something in between.
• **Need to Know:** The info you need to make your trip run smoothly, including getting about by public transport, weather tips, emergency phone numbers and useful websites.

Navigation In the Tenerife by Area chapter, we've given each area its own colour, which is also used on the locator maps throughout the book and the map on the inside front cover.

Maps The fold-out map accompanying this book is a comprehensive map of Tenerife and La Gomera. The grid on this fold-out map is the same as the grid on the locator maps within the book. The grid references to these maps are shown with capital letters, for example A1. The grid references to the town plan are shown with lower-case letters, for example a1.

Contents

CONTENTS

Introducing Tenerife

Mention Tenerife and most people think immediately of warm sun and beaches, and perhaps also of the lively resorts catering to sun-seekers who are drawn from northern winters to its year-round spring climate.

But Tenerife is so much more. Soaring cliffs rise straight out of the sea, so steeply that entire sections of the coast have no road access. Although the island is a scant 96.5km (60 miles) from end to end, its centre rises to the highest peak in Spain—Mount Teide, at 3,718m (12,195ft).

Below the cone of this still-sizzling volcano lies a crater some 17km (11 miles) across, filled with fantastic landscapes of coloured rock and volcanic sand dunes. Mountain ranges spread out to the east and west, and some of Europe's most spectacular drives are along their spines. Just below the highest elevations, pine forests colour the mountainsides deep green.

From these central and smaller volcanoes flow occasional swaths of rough black lava, flows that have in the past—even as recently as the 1700s—destroyed towns and left long stretches of the northern coast rimmed with black uneven rock. Where beaches lie between them, they are usually made of fine black sand; the beautiful golden strands on the south coast have been created from sand purposefully brought from the Sahara.

Along with the holiday havens where most visitors soak up rays, Tenerife has gracious old towns founded by the Spanish who colonized the island in the 1500s. Church spires of volcanic stone and white stucco rise above streets lined by carved wooden balconies. Where locals have not planted gardens, wild flowers spring up.

Tenerife is full of these surprises, and discovering them is more than half the fun of a holiday in these very well-named 'Fortunate Isles.'

Facts + Figures

- **Area of island: 2,035sq km (786sq miles)**
- **Population: 850,000**
- **Tenerife has five Denomination of Origin wine regions**

PROTECTED NATURAL AREAS

In addition to the national park, Tenerife has 42 designated nature reserves, natural monuments and protected natural spaces. The largest of these are the Corona Forestal—the pine forest that surrounds the crater of Teide—and the Anaga Rural Park.

ISLAND ARCHITECTURE

Buildings remain from all eras of island history since the early 1500s, and most are well preserved. Santa Cruz, La Orotava, La Laguna and Puerto de la Cruz have churches dating from the early years of Spanish settlement, and a number of fine old homes from the 1600s survive. Traditional wooden balconies, both outside and around their characteristic interior patios, are the hallmarks of these buildings.

TRAIL NETWORK

Tenerife has a network of 22 designated walking routes across the island. These range in length from two-hour walks to six-hour rambles. A free map of the routes is available in tourist offices, giving details such as length, gradient, difficulty and even each walk's degree of cultural and natural interest.

A Short Stay in Tenerife

DAY 1: SANTA CRUZ

Morning Begin your day early in Santa Cruz at the busy **Mercado Nuestra Señora de África** (▷ 32–33), where you can find a café for breakfast. Then head for the nearby **Museo de la Naturaleza y el Hombre** (▷ 34–35), when the doors open at 9am. No single place gives a better introduction to the island, with exhibits on both its human and natural history, beginning with its violent volcanic past.

Mid-morning Cross the footbridge to the historic church of **Nuestra Señora de Concepción** (▷ 42).

Lunch In front of the church is a pedestrianized street known as La Noria, at whose far end are nearly a dozen casual restaurants (▷ 47–48).

Afternoon Take in two of the city's most striking works of modern architecture (take the Tranvia tram one stop from Fundacion to the central station or walk along Avenida de la Constitución), Santiago Calatrava's Auditorio and **Parque Marítimo César Manrique** (▷ 36–37).

Mid-afternoon If you planned ahead and brought a swimsuit, Parque Marítimo César Manrique is a good place to cool off; if you didn't bring one, it's still a nice place to catch some sun and have a refreshing drink.

Dinner Treat yourself to a traditional Canarian dinner at local favourite **La Hierbita** (▷ 48), not far from Nuestra Señora de Concepción.

Evening Head back to the Auditorio for a performance, or if your taste runs to disco, continue on to Las Cascadas, in the building that seems to cascade into Parque Marítimo, to dance at **Dreams Tenerife** (▷ 46).

DAY 2: TEIDE NATIONAL PARK

Morning Begin your day at 8.30, heading by car along the TS21 or by TITSA bus 342 or 348 to the crater of Las Cañadas, in **Teide National Park** (▷ 66–67).

Mid-morning Depending on your sightseeing preferences, either follow the trail around Los Roques de Garcia to see amazing rock and lava formations (▷ 67), or, if it's a clear day, ride the Teleférico (▷ 67) to just below the summit for limitless views.

Lunch The **Parador de Cañadas del Teide**, inside the crater near Los Roques, has a cafeteria (▷ 111) with a terrace.

Afternoon If you are interested in seeing still more of the crater, do whichever morning activity you skipped. Otherwise head down the north side, stopping to see the displays and garden of indigenous plants from the crater at the visitor centre. Continue, following the winding road through the pine forest of Corona Forestal to **La Orotava** (▷ 64–65).

Mid-afternoon Stop at the tourist office for a map and use it to locate some of the fine old homes with their distinctive carved balconies. End with a stroll through the terraced **Jardines Marquesado de la Quinta Roja** (▷ 68).

Dinner Consider dining early at **Bodegon de los Compadres**, a typical Canarian restaurant (▷ 74).

Evening If you began at the south coast, head back via the motorways TF5 and TF1. If you began on the north coast, continue on to Puerto de la Cruz to hear a little Canarian music at **El Arado** (▷ 73).

Top 25

▶▶▶

Jardín Acuático Risco Bello,
Jardín Botánico,
Lago Martiánco
Puerto de la Cruz

Garachico

**Drago Milenario &
Icod de los Vinos**

Loro
Parque

La
Orotava

**THE WEST
49–74**

3718
El Teide

Parque Nacional
del Teide

**Acantilados
de los Gigantes**

Vilaflor

Playa de las
Américas

Los Cristianos

**THE SOUTH
75–90**

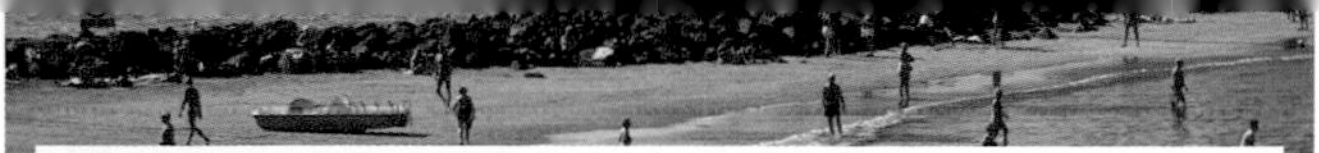

These pages are a quick guide to the Top 25, which are described in more detail later. Here they are listed alphabetically, and the tinted background shows which area they are in.

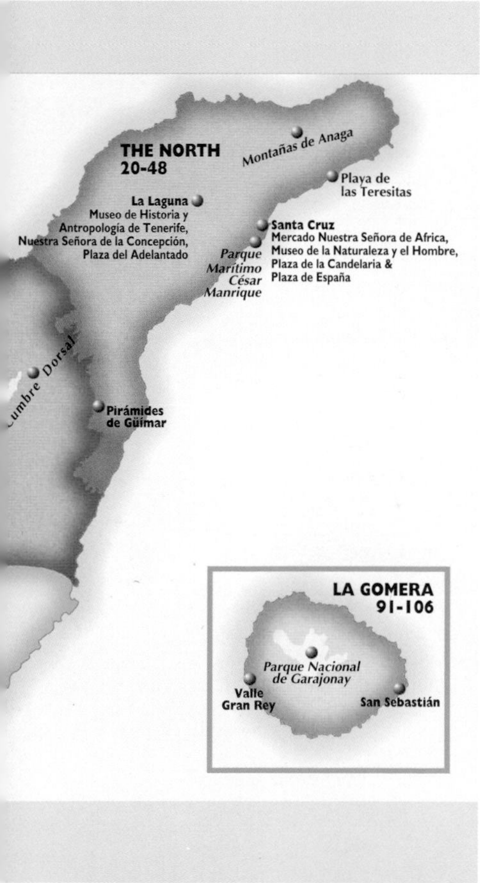

THE NORTH
20–48

Montañas de Anaga

Playa de las Teresitas

La Laguna
Museo de Historia y Antropología de Tenerife,
Nuestra Señora de la Concepción,
Plaza del Adelantado

Santa Cruz
Mercado Nuestra Señora de Africa,
Museo de la Naturaleza y el Hombre,
Plaza de la Candelaria &
Plaza de España

Parque Marítimo César Manrique

Cumbre Dorsal

Pirámides de Güímar

LA GOMERA
91–106

Parque Nacional de Garajonay

Valle Gran Rey

San Sebastián

ESSENTIAL TENERIFE TOP 25

◀ ◀ ◀

9

Beaches

Travellers looking for sun and sand generally head for the south coast, where
lively resort enclaves have grown behind
a stretch of man-made beaches bathed
in sunlight almost 365 days a year. Los
Cristianos and Playa de las Américas
(▷ 78–79) are most people's vision of
Tenerife, a coast bordered in wide beaches
of golden sand.

The South Coast

Los Cristianos' relaxed family-oriented clientele
enjoy the golden sands of Playa de las Vistas,
and a series of beaches extends to the manicured enclaves around Playa del Duque, on
the Costa Adeje to the west. Smaller natural
(dark sand) beaches dot the entire shore east
of Los Cristianos to El Medano, just east of
Tenerife Sur Airport. Too windy for comfortable sunbathing and with seas too rough for
swimming, El Medano is a world-class surfing
beach. Farther west the coast swings north
to Playa Santiago (▷ 52), which is small, but
among of the island's nicest natural beaches.
Nearby Playa de la Arena is backed by a park
of palms and flowers and protected by rocky
headlands. The island's longest and loveliest
beach is another imported from Africa, Playa
de las Teresitas (▷ 31), used mostly by locals
from nearby Santa Cruz. Its golden sands are
protected by artificial barrier reefs that give the
beach a gradual slope, making it perfect for
children, snorkellers and swimmers who don't

A GOOD USE FOR SAHARA SAND

Tenerife's volcanic history means that its natural sand
beaches are not the golden strands of topical isle fame.
The volcanic sand is dark gray at best, almost black in
places. But only a short distance away is an inexhaustible
supply of golden sand, so Canarians have simply brought
some of the Sahara to their shores, building reefs of the
coarse volcanic rock to keep the tides from washing the
new beaches away. Playa de las Teresitas is the largest of
these, at 1.5km (1 mile) long.

*From top: Windsurfer; El
Médano; pavement detail,
Playa de las Américas; sun-
rise, Playa de las Teresitas*

like the heavy surf of some of the region's other beaches.

Northern Beaches

On the other side of the Anaga mountains on the north coast are the beaches of Taganana (▷ 44), including some with good surfing and a long stretch of sand at Benijo kept remote by the steep cliff path required to access it. Puerto de la Cruz's main beach, Playa Jardín (▷ 70) is a long strand with palms and gardens, one of the few sandy beaches on the north shore. It was designed by architect César Manrique, better known for adapting the island's rocky coast into swimming parks, such as the one nearby at Lago Martiánez (▷ 59). Much of the northern shore is rough black lava that has been worn into tidal pools by the pounding surf. Manrique turned these pools into eye-catching parks with swimming pools and sun terraces set into the natural shore. Manrique's work may have inspired the smaller sea park at Garachico (▷ 56), where a beautiful recrea-tion area is built around natural seawater pools in the lava that engulfed the harbor 300 years ago. Elsewhere the pools are left to their natu-ral state, as along the shore between Bajamar and Punta del Hidalgo (▷ 41). Used mostly by locals (although anyone is welcome), these rocky shores have small patches of sand, natural wading pools and the serenity that the beautiful beaches can seldom offer.

From top: Punta del Hidalgo; pool, Bajamar; Playa de las Américas; café; Anaga peninsula coastline

LA GOMERA'S BEACHES

La Gomera is not famous for its beaches, although sandy strands are not altogether missing. The island's longest is right in the capital of San Sebastián (▷ 96–97), and a smaller one is reached by a tunnel through the headland, right at the ferry port. At the far end of Valle Gran Rey (▷ 98–99), the beach at Playa Inglés is a mix of pools, black sand and dramatic outcrops of black lava below towering cliffs. Bathing here is clothing-optional. At the other end of town is a small sandy beach with gentler sea, at the fishing and ferry harbour.

Shopping

Between local handicrafts, duty-free goods, beachwear, good things to eat and the 'citified' shops of Calle Castillo and El Corte Ingles in Santa Cruz, there is plenty of reason to shop on Tenerife.

What to Buy

Tenerife is known for its lace—appropriately called Tenerife work or Tenerife lace (▷ panel, below). You'll find pulled thread borders on table linens, clothing and pillowcases. If you want genuine Tenerife work, buy from a reputable shop and be prepared to pay a fair price for the labour-intensive craftmanship. Pottery is another local speciality, especially interesting because it is one of the few skills that has changed little since pre-colonial times. Perfectly symmetrical dishes and vessels are shaped by hand without a wheel. Also look out for items woven or appliquéd from banana leaves, such as baskets, table mats and dolls.

Where to Shop

The lively resorts are lined with shops, especially Los Cristianos, Playa de las Américas and Puerto de la Cruz, which also have shopping malls. In the upscale Baia del Duque area of Costa Adeje is a circular multistorey shoppers' nirvana complete with car park and a play areas for children. The shops match the tone of the surrounding resorts, concentrating on high fashion and jewellery. Major resorts also have weekly or semi-weekly street markets.

TENERIFE LACE

There are actually two types known by this name. Tenerife lace is, properly, lace made on a round pin-cushion, creating small circles. These are used as doilies or cup coasters or sewn together into table linens or trims for clothing. But the intricate drawn thread work called *calados* is also a Tenerife speciality. In this style, several rows of threads are removed from woven fabric and the remaining cross threads are needle-woven into intricate designs to form lacy bands.

From top: traditional pots; leather bags; El Cercado pottery, La Gomera; straw hats

Tenerife by Night

Nightlife begins late, not surprising since islanders eat late by northern European standards. Clubs and pubs frequented by locals begin to fill around 10pm or 11pm and still are going strong long after midnight. The hottest scenes are in Santa Cruz and La Laguna, where university students keep things lively and late.

Evening Entertainment

On the south coast, Las Américas and the Baia del Duque area have the most serious nightlife, but every resort has its hot spots. Puerto de la Cruz is a bit more sedate; in the evening and well into the night people congregate around the large Plaza del Charco, filled with bars, cafes and restaurants. The seafront promenades like Puerto de la Cruz's Paseo San Telmo are usually well lit and filled with people strolling at night. In smaller towns, such as La Orotava, nightlife is more likely to be dinner in a convivial bodega, where locals and visitors mix easily. Fiestas are common occurrences, bringing everyone to the streets—a good opportunity to join in the fun.

Santa Cruz

As befits the island capital, Santa Cruz has a full schedule of musical and other performances. Classical, jazz and world music are performed in the Auditorio and just beyond it, above Parque Marítimo, is a complex that includes Dreams, a disco that attracts top world performers and groups (▷ 46).

The hottest nightlife is in the south of the island, around Playa de las Américas

---

CARNIVAL

Each February, Santa Cruz and Puerto de la Cruz—joined by the whole island—go wild. Only Rio de Janeiro outdoes the colourful, fanciful and fantastic costumes, bands, parades and general pandemonium that takes over the capital. Shrove Tuesday is the biggest day, with processions that seem to include everyone on the island. Hotels are reserved well in advance by people from all over the Spanish-speaking world.

Eating Out

Dining out is a treat on Tenerife, where local chefs have long appreciated the ingredients produced by local farms, dairies and vineyards. While the word 'localvore' may be unfamiliar, the concept was popular here long before it became fashionable.

Canarian Cuisine

While the array of international cuisines found at resorts is staggering, be sure to dine at least once in a typical Canarian restaurant to sample local specialties. Starters will certainly include *papas arrugadas,* small boiled potatoes with a salty crust, served with two *mojos*—sauces of red peppers and of coriander leaves. Shrimp sizzling in olive oil and garlic is another favourite, as are *pimientos padron*—small green peppers fried and sprinkled with sea salt. Most are sweet, an occasional hot one makes them exciting to eat. For mains, seafood is nearly always on the menu. Pork and chicken are standards, with rabbit and goat also common.

Dress and Mealtimes

Even in high-end restaurants dress is usually casual, although beachwear is welcome only at beach bars. Canarians themselves tend to be casual in resort areas, but do dress up a bit in Santa Cruz or at more formal dining venues. Locals rarely wear shorts when they go out to dinner. Although islanders dine late—about 9pm—restaurateurs are used to northern European tastes and in resort areas open as early as 5.30pm.

BUSY BEES

Canary Island bees produce some of the world's finest honey (*miel*), although it is little known outside the islands. Some of the flowers they visit grow only here, and the flavours subtly reflect these exotic blossoms. The three most popular Tenerife honeys are Miel de Retama from broom blossoms, Miel de Tajineste from bugloss and Miel de Brezal from heather. Find these at farmers' markets and shops specializing in local foods (▷ 45).

From top: Café terrace, El Sauzal; seafood; outdoor dining table; honey for sale

Restaurants by Cuisine

While traditional Canarian cuisine is by far the most common on the island, resort areas and cities offer a wider variety. Here restaurants are listed according to the foods they specialize in, with page references for more detailed information.

CAFÉS AND ICE CREAM

Café Capriccio (▷ 47)
Il Caffe di Roma (▷ 47)
Heladería La Flor de Alicante (▷ 48)
Oh La Lá (▷ 48)

CANARIAN

Bodega San Sebastián (▷ 47)
Bodegon de los Compadres (▷ 74)
Bulan (▷ 47)
Casa Conchita (▷ 106)
Casa Tita (▷ 47)
La Caseta (▷ 47)
Cuatro Caminos (▷ 106)
Fonda Central (▷ 90)
La Hierbita (▷ 48)
El Jable (▷ 90)
Laguna Grande (▷ 106)
Otelo (▷ 90)
Restaurante Juonia (▷ 106)
Restaurante Sanchez (▷ 48)
Taberna Ramon (▷ 48)

Terraza El Mirador La Calera (▷ 106)
El Tcrrcro (▷ 90)
Victoria Restaurante & Tasca (▷ 74)

CONTINENTAL SPAIN

Don Pelayo (▷ 47)
Restaurante – Cafeteria Olympo (▷ 48)
Tasca Sáfron y El Porrón (▷ 48)

CREATIVE CUISINE

Escondida (▷ 74)
Mil Sabores (▷ 74)
Restaurante Regulo (▷ 74)
La Rosa di Bari (▷ 74)
Tasquita Pimenton (▷ 90)

GRILLS AND MEAT SPECIALTIES

Asador Portillo (▷ 90)
Bodegon Matias (▷ 74)
Chiringo Atlantico (▷ 90)
España (▷ 90)

Martínez (▷ 48)
La Palmita (▷ 106)
El Paraiso (▷ 106)

OTHER CUISINES

Café Arena (▷ 74)
La Cazuela (▷ 47)
La Cueva (▷ 90)
El Inti (▷ 90)
Mirabello Restaurante (▷ 90)

SEAFOOD

Casa Juana (▷ 74)
Castillo del Mar (▷ 106)
Charco del Conde (▷ 106)
Los Churritos Casa Fernando (▷ 47)
Cofradia de Pescadores (▷ 47)
El Pejin (▷ 106)
Restaurante Rustico (▷ 74)

If You Like...

However you'd like to spend your time in Tenerife, these ideas should help you tailor your perfect visit. Each suggestion has a fuller write-up elsewhere in the book.

SHOPPING FOR LOCAL CRAFTS

Step onto the patio of Casa de los Balcones (▷ 64) in La Orotava to watch Tenerife drawn-thread work demonstrated.
Spend Saturday morning at Mercadillo del Agricultor y Artesano (▷ 45) in Tegueste.
Browse the juried selection at Artenerife's kiosk (▷ 72) in Puerto de la Cruz.
Take home a whimsical wooden puzzle from Essenza Arte y Artesanias (▷ 72) in Puerto de la Cruz.

Lacework, La Orotava

DINING IN HISTORIC SETTINGS

Choose a table next to the stone fountain on the patio of Restaurante Regulo (▷ 74) in Puerto de la Cruz.
Step back to the 16th century at Victoria Restaurante & Tasca (▷ 74) in Puerto de la Cruz.
Absorb the atmosphere of a distin-guished colonial home over dinner at El Terrero (▷ 90) in Granadilla.

Tasty cuisine

SEA VIEWS WITH YOUR SEAFOOD

Watch the boats that just brought your dinner ashore, at Cofradia de Pescadores (▷ 47) in Punta del Hidalgo.
Dine with a different view of the same coast, at La Caseta (▷ 47).
Watch waves crash on the lava rocks below the terrace of Restaurante Rustico (▷ 74) in Puerto de la Cruz.
See Teide's cone across the sea from Castillo del Mar (▷ 106) on La Gomera.

Café, Playa de las Américas

LIVE MUSIC

Classical music

Catch a hot European group at Dreams Tenerife (▷ 46) in Santa Cruz.

Stop after dinner for a *chupito* and Canarian music at El Arado (▷ 73) in Puerto de la Cruz.

Check what's on at Tenerife Palace (▷ 73) in Puerto de la Cruz—it could be ballet or a rock band.

Absorb some culture in Playa de las Américas with dinner and chamber music at La Piramide (▷ 89).

HAPPY KIDS

Camel, Camello Center

Meet mummies—real ones—at the Museo de la Naturaleza y el Hombre (▷ 34–35) in Santa Cruz.

Watch dolphins cavort and pelicans fish at Loro Parque (▷ 58).

Ride a camel at the Camello Center (▷ 68).

Build castles from Sahara sand at Playa de las Teresitas (▷ 31).

Get wet at Aqualand (▷ 82).

ONLY THE BEST

Browse for baubles at Plaza Playa del Duque (▷ 78–79) in Costa Adeje.

Book a spa day when you book your suite at Gran Hotel Bahía del Duque (▷ 112).

Hear a world-class orchestra in the Auditorio (▷ 36–37) designed by Spain's premier architect.

Savour the freshest local ingredients at Mil Sabores (▷ 74) in Puerto de la Cruz.

Munch on the island's best *pimientos padron* (fried peppers) at Tasquita Pimenton (▷ 90) in Arico el Nuevo.

Gran Hotel Bahía del Duque

TASTING WINES

Arrange a private vineyard tour at Bodegas Monje (▷ 46) in El Sauzal.

Visit the tasting room of Bodega San Sebastián (▷ 47) in Santa Cruz.

Sample local wines and cheeses in the bodega of La Orotava's Casa Lercaro (▷ 64).

Try wines from Europe's highest vineyards at the bodegas of Lajial and Zeveron in Vilaflor (▷ 80–81).

Local wine, Tacoronte

PRE-COLONIAL HISTORY

Ponder the mysteries of Pirámides de Güímar (▷ 30).

Peek into a Guanche burial cave at the Museo Arqueológico (▷ 70) in Puerto de la Cruz.

Pick up a free hiking guide and explore the Guanche caves of Chiñama in Granadilla de Abona (▷ 83).

Meet archaeologists studying the island's first inhabitants, at the Museo Arqueológico de La Gomera (▷ 101) in San Sebastián.

Guanche statue, Güímar

TRAILS UNDER YOUR BOOTS

Circle Roques de García in Teide National Park (▷ 66–67).

Hike into the Anaga Mountains (▷ 28–29) from Punta del Hidalgo.

Follow a track from the Cumbre Dorsal (▷ 53) for ever-changing views of El Teide.

Be one of 200 walkers admitted each day to Barranco del Infierno (▷ 82) in Adeje.

Walk in the laurel forest of Garajonay National Park (▷ 94–95) on La Gomera.

El Teide (above); Calle del Castillo, Santa Cruz (below)

VALUE FOR MONEY

Relax and enjoy sea views from your apartment's big balcony at Finca Vista Bonita (▷ 109) in San Miguel.

Kick back by the pool overlooking Puerto de la Cruz at Acuario (▷ 109).

Shop on Calle Castillo in Santa Cruz, then drop in at Hotel Pelinor (▷ 110), a block away.

Tenerife by Area

THE NORTH

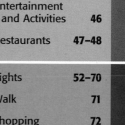

THE WEST

THE SOUTH

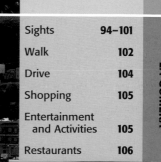

LA GOMERA

The North

From its lively and urbane capital and the genteel, historic streets of La Laguna to the remote and wild Anaga mountain range and the golden sands of Tenerife's best beach, the northern part of the island is a study in contrasts.

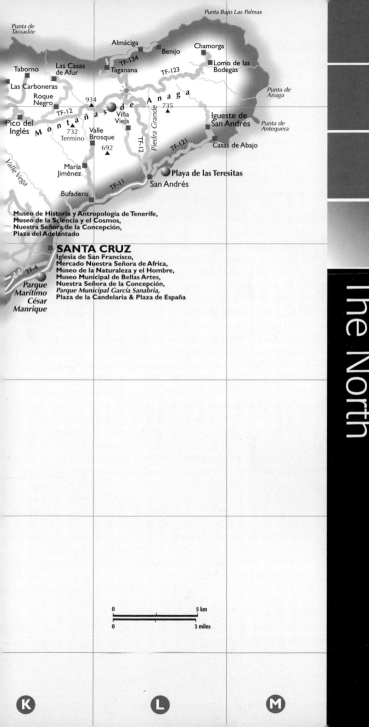

Punta Bajo Las Palmas

Punta de Tamadite

Almáciga

Chamorga

Benijo

Taborno

Las Casas de Afur

Taganana

TF-134

Lomo de las Bodegas

TF-123

Las Carboneras

Roque Negro

TF-12

934

M o n t a ñ a s   d e   A n a g a

Punta de Anaga

Pico del Inglés

732 Termino

Viña Vieja

735

Igueste de San Andrés

Punta de Antequera

Valle Brosque

Piedra Grande

Casas de Abajo

TF-12

692

TF-121

Valle Vega

Maria Jiménez

TF-11

Playa de las Teresitas

San Andrés

Bufadero

Museo de Historia y Antropología de Tenerife,
Museo de la Sciencia y el Cosmos,
Nuestra Señora de la Concepción,
Plaza del Adelantado

TF-4

SANTA CRUZ
Iglesia de San Francisco,
Mercado Nuestra Señora de Africa,
Museo de la Naturaleza y el Hombre,
Museo Municipal de Bellas Artes,
Nuestra Señora de la Concepción,
Parque Municipal García Sanabria,
Plaza de la Candelaria & Plaza de España

Parque
Marítimo
César
Manrique

0   5 km

0   3 miles

K

L

M

La Laguna: Museo de Historia y Antropología

TOP 25

Model fishing boat (left); carved balcony on the outside of the Casa Lercaro (right)

THE BASICS

www.museosdetenerife.org

✚ J2

✉ Casa Lercaro, Calle San Agustín 20–22, La Laguna

☎ 922 82 59 49, 922 82 59 43

🕐 Tue–Sun 9–7

👆 Inexpensive

🍴 Several nearby

🚌 TITSA buses 016, 105 and Tranvia 'La Trinidad'

♿ Few

HIGHLIGHTS

● Lercaro mansion architecture
● Cartography collections
● Religious history exhibits
● Maritime history exhibits

Unlike many history museums that deal only with the more remote past, Tenerife's brings the very recent past to life as well, so presenting the full range of the island's story since Spanish settlement.

Noble mansion Located in La Laguna in the Casa Lercaro, built by an Italian family in the 16th century, its collections are a trove of articles and documents detailing the conquest and development of the island since the 1490s. The mansion itself is well restored and makes the transition to a museum without losing its character. The gracious noble home is in the traditional configuration around a courtyard; wooden balconies carved in intricate detail surround this patio, supported by stone columns. To bring the house into the context of the museum, an entire exhibit is dedicated to the Lercaro family.

Exhibits and collections Collections in the museum are especially strong in the Spanish conquest and early years when the monasteries and churches were founded. The island's maritime history gets full attention as well, appropriate because of its significant location as a staging point for the Spanish explorations of the new world. Historical maps form one permanent exhibit. A full schedule of events, classes in historic arts and theatrical performances interpret historical themes. There are more exhibits at the Casa de Carta (▷ 40), formerly the separate Museo de Antropología, in Valle de Guerra.

TOP 25

La Laguna: Nuestra Señora de la Concepción

Tenerife's mother church holds some of the greatest Spanish cultural jewels of the island. Other than its tower, the exterior is undistinguished: the interior holds the treasures.

Gothic to baroque While the Spanish, under Fernández de Lugo, had invaded and settled into Santa Cruz in 1494, it was not until Christmas Day 1495 that the Guanche kings were beaten at the second battle of Acentejo in what was to become La Laguna. The first parish church on the island was established there in 1496, and the present church erected a few years later. It was declared a Spanish National Treasure in 1947. With roots in the Gothic, the church has been enhanced over the centuries and shows touches of the Renaissance and baroque.

Treasures within One of the primary treasures is the hand-carved cedar pulpit carved by the French sculptor Verau in the 18th century. The Seville baptismal font, to one side of the main entrance, was allegedly used in the baptism of defeated Guanche warriors and dates from the 15th century. The artwork within the church includes statues and paintings of Christ and saints done by European and Canarian artists during the half-millennia of the church's existence.

Climb for views The four-storey tower outside the entrance dates from the 17th century. There's a security gate inside the door, but visitors can climb the tower for a view over the city.

THE BASICS

✚ J2

✉ Plaza de la Concepción, La Laguna

🕐 Mon–Fri 8.30–1.45, 5.30–7.30, Sat 8.30–1.45, 5–7.30, Sun 7.30–1.45, 4.30–8.30

🚌 TITSA buses 102, 107, 108, Tranvia from Santa Cruz 'La Trinidad'

♿ Few

HIGHLIGHTS

● Carved wooden nave ceiling
● 15th-century Spanish font
● 18th-century cedar pulpit
● 17th-century tower

La Laguna: Plaza del Adelantado

While the patrician streets of La Laguna's historic quarter are rarely bustling, the Plaza del Adelantado offers a welcome and peaceful rest from the rigours of sightseeing, its benches shaded by mature old trees.

Grand surroundings The leafy square is a good vantage point for admiring the façades around it, as well for enjoying the Carrara marble fountain in its centre. Among the buildings that look out onto the square are the neoclassical Ayuntamiento (town hall), the church and convent of Santa Catalina (where mothers were able to leave unwanted baby girls in former times), the Nava palace, the court building and the little Ermita de San Miguel. Morning visitors can join locals in the market, which also faces the plaza. Behind the

Court house, Plaza del Adelantado (left); Ermita de San Miguel (middle); the trees make the square a shady retreat (right)

town hall stretches the long Casa de los Capitanes Generales, dating from 1624, in whose inner courtyard is a sparse tourist office. A smaller, but much more informative kiosk is tucked in a niche next to Nuestra Señora de la Concepción.

World heritage The richest legacy of La Laguna's architecture, which won the old quarter's UNESCO World Heritage Site designation, lies in the streets between Plaza del Adelantado and the church of Nuestra Señora de la Concepción (▷ 25). In this area are the 16th-century cathedral (with an outstanding marble pulpit), three other churches and a clutch of noble homes, several of which are open for view as museums, public offices or even a hotel. In the midst of this, a distinguished 'modern' building, the 1915 Teatro Leal (▷ 46), faces Calle Obisbo Rey Redondo.

THE BASICS

✚ J2

✉ La Laguna

🚌 TITSA bus 016, 105; Tranvia 'La Trinidad'

🍴 Few

♿ Few

❓ Free tours in English Mon–Fri at 11am by reservation

ℹ Calle Obisbo Redondo 1, tel 922 63 11 94; Mon–Fri 9–5, Sat–Sun 9–3

Montañas de Anaga

Rocky coastline (left); walking trails (right); view from Mirador Pico del Inglés (opposite)

THE BASICS

✚ K2–L1

Visitor Centre
✉ Cruz de Carmen, TF 12
☎ 922 633 576
🕑 Oct–Jun daily 9.30–4,
Jul–Sep daily 9.30–3
🚌 TITSA buses 073, 075,
076, 077
♿ Very good
🎟 Free

HIGHLIGHTS

● Mirador Pico del Inglés
● Cruz de Carmen
● Taganana
● Walking at least one
trail (with an illustrated
guide/map)

TIPS

● The loop trail at Cruz de
Carmen is a good choice for
learning about the paths that
once connected villages.
● Along with Cruz de
Carmen, the tourist office in
Punta Hidalgo is the most
informative for hikers.

Parque Rural Anaga protects Tenerife's northeast tip, which, although close to the capital, is still little visited by tourists. Any road or trail into these mountains will bring grand views and a look at a timeless way of life.

Dramatic driving Not the island's tallest mountains—the Anagas are only about 1,000m (3,300ft) at their highest point—they are every bit as dramatic as the better-known peaks to the west. They form a sharp ridge (*cumbre*) in the centre, a spine so sharp that the road narrows to one lane in places, with simultaneous views to the sea almost directly below on either side. The northern shore is so steep that only two short sections—at Taganana and Punta Hidalgo—have road access. Hiking trails form a network, following both ridges and the *barrancos* between them, and excellent free trail maps describe these in detail.

Scenic stops Miradors overlook the jagged peaks and deep valleys at several points, giving drivers a chance to see what lies below, and providing access to footpaths. Mirador Pico del Inglés, on a shoulder of Mount Taborno, is the most spectacular. Cruz de Carmen's visitor centre is a good first stop, to learn about the flora, fauna, geology and way of life for people who settled in these forbidding mountains. The small museum shows how forests change with altitude (ask for the free illustrated tree guide), and displays Guanche artifacts. Photo panels on village life, beliefs, crafts and work have English translations.

Pirámides de Güímar

Replica of Ra II (left); statue in the museum (middle); stepped pyramid (right)

THE BASICS

www.piramidesdeguimar.net

+ H5
- ✉ Calle Chacona, Güímar
- ☎ 922 51 45 10
- 🕐 Daily 9.30–6
- 🍴 Café (€)
- 🚌 TITSA bus 120
- ♿ Excellent
- 💷 Expensive

HIGHLIGHTS

● Heyerdahl documentary on the movement of peoples
● Gardens of indigenous plants
● Models and replicas of Heyerdahl's boats *Kon-Tiki*, *Ra* and *Ra II*

Do these stone pyramids help unlock the secrets shared by the pharaohs and the Mayans, or are they simply farmers' terraces? Thor Heyerdahl spent his last years here unravelling this riddle.

Almost lost A newspaper article in 1990 saved this ancient site from destruction, bringing internationally known student of human migrations, Thor Heyerdahl, to Tenerife to explore the series of terraced platforms described in the article.

Pyramid power While Heyerdahl's theories of migration are controversial, his work and that of archaeologists at this site show clear similarities with pyramids around the world. The site is known to have been occupied by Guanches (the original island inhabitants), but there is no record of the construction of the pyramid complex, whose three main structures and open fields bear an uncanny resemblance to South American temple complexes. These pyramids have also been shown to align with the winter and summer solstices. And the construction is far more precise than the old terraces used by local farmers.

Unravelling the past An excellent documentary in the auditorium and exhibits in the Casa Chacona Museum provide more information on the temple structures of sun-worshippers and on the local Guanche culture. A separate mini-museum explains the voyages that Heyerdahl took in pursuit of his theories, and includes models of his ancient craft and a full-sized replica of *Ra II*.

Playa de las Teresitas at sunrise (left); looking down the beach to San Andrés (right)

Playa de las Teresitas

Like resort beaches on the south coast, Playa de las Teresitas is made of fine golden sand imported from the Sahara, but unlike them was built for locals—though they are happy to share.

The Sahara's best Lying 2km (1 mile) outside San Andrés, and only 9km (5.5 miles) from Santa Cruz, is the islanders' favourite beach, a 1.5km-long (1-mile) crescent of golden sand protected by artificial barrier reefs. These reefs partially enclose a lagoon with a long, gradual incline into the water, making it ideal for children, snorkellers and swimmers wary of the open sea that buffets many other parts of the coast.

Join the islanders Palms and other trees offer some welcome shade, and amenities include umbrellas and beach chairs for hire, free changing rooms (*vestuarias*) and snack kiosks evenly spaced along the beach, and plentiful parking. A steep headland rises sharply at one end, while the pleasant fishing town of San Andrés is at the other, with plenty of good seafood restaurants. Perhaps the most charming thing about las Teresitas is its free-flowing casual atmosphere. There are no regimented lines of resort-reserved lounges here—just the appealing helter-skelter of chairs, blankets and towels that marks hometown beaches everywhere. Locals wait patiently for their turn at a shower or changing cabana, greeting each other and total strangers cordially. It's not only the island's most beautiful beach, it's a slice of local life.

THE BASICS

L2
TF121, San Andrés
Kiosks on beach, restaurants in San Andrés
TITSA bus 910
Few
 Free

HIGHLIGHTS

- Fine golden sand
- Protected swimming water
- Snorkelling
- Gradual drop-off for child safety

Santa Cruz: Mercado Nuestra Señora de África

TOP
25

HIGHLIGHTS

● Sampling Canary Islands cheeses, hard to find elsewhere
● Colourful flower market
● Leghera Canaria statue
● Sunday flea market

The market is a good way to absorb contemporary Canarian culture. Everyone comes here: your chef for dinner tonight was probably here this morning—and so were the flowers on your table.

Grand entrance Built by the Franco regime in the 1940s, the outside of the atmospheric market has a definite North African feel to it. Inside it is a riot of commerce. This is where the people of Santa Cruz buy their fresh vegetables, fruits and popular locally produced meats like rabbit and goat. Outside its wide arched entrance stands the bronze statue of *Leghera Canaria* by Compan y Zamoramo Guzman.

Cheeses aplenty If you are not aware of the joys of Canarian cheeses this is the place to

Clockwise from left: Market entrance; tempting arrays of local fruit and vegetables; bananas and chillies; exotic blooms

become friends with them. There are many great Canarian cheeses like the hard Tofio cheeses with rinds encased in *gofio* or sharp tangy paprika called *pimenton*. Softer, more subtle goat and sheep cheeses, some unflavoured and others artfully enhanced with local herbs, can also be sampled and bought here.

Flowers to fish The stalls in the patio of the enclosed market include brilliant flowers and plants, while downstairs are the butcher and fishmonger sections. Look too for all sorts of other wares from handcrafts to sellers of locally produced music, one of the best souvenirs. On Sundays there is no official market but a large flea market, the Rastro, take place on the streets outside, with a seemingly endless assortment of new and second-hand goods.

THE BASICS

www.mercado-municipal.com

⊞ c4

✉ Avenida San Sebastián, Santa Cruz

☎ 922 21 47 43

⏰ Daily 6–3

🍴 Café (€)

🚃 Tranvia 'Guimera'

♿ Few

🆓 Free

Santa Cruz: Museo de la Naturaleza y el Hombre

TOP 25

HIGHLIGHTS

● Guanche mummies
● Sealife collections
● Formation of the islands galleries

TIPS

● Show a TITSA BONOBUS voucher for a 50 per cent discount.
● Divide your tour into two visits—tickets allow a return later the same day.

Two outstanding museums in one, the Museum of Nature and Man, with its bright and engaging collection of exhibits, would be a cultural credit to a city many times the size of Santa Cruz.

Bringing the past to life Visitors curious about the Canary Islands—from their volcanic formation to the people, creatures and flora that inhabit them now—should not miss this outstanding series of exhibits, displayed in an attractive former hospital. One could easily break the experience into two separate visits, one for the natural history wing and one for the human history and culture of the land. Visitors interested in the pre-Spanish history and inhabitants of the archipelago should come here to identify Guanche sites to explore

Clockwise from left: Clear display cases in the Museum of Nature; the elegant neoclassical façade of the building; outdoor sculpture; ceramic pots; one of the former hospital's quiet courtyards

on all the islands—especially as information on these is often lacking in tourism offices.

Real mummies Although children will find few interactive exhibits, they will find something far more exciting—real mummies. The Guanches mummified their dead and despite efforts of the early religious orders to destroy all vestiges of these, a few survived and are arrestingly displayed and well interpreted here. As interesting are the exhibits showing how skeletons can tell historians about the life, work, diseases and diet of long-ago peoples. See the sealife exhibits in Area 3 before embarking on a whale watch, and look for examples of some of the sea creatures you may find on your plate—though hopefully not the giant squid suspended overhead.

Santa Cruz: Parque Marítimo César Manrique

HIGHLIGHTS

● A concert at the Auditorio
● Swimming and sunbathing at Parque Marítimo
● Manrique sculpture in plaza

TIPS

● Book ahead to take a guided tour of the Auditorio, including hidden corners rarely seen by the public.
● For an unusual perspective of the Auditorio, usually photographed from the side, try shooting it head on.

In very few places can you stand in full view of works by two cutting-edge modern architects. In Santa Cruz you can even swim in one all afternoon, then attend a concert in the other in the evening.

Urban playground If Parque Marítimo is one of César Manrique's least-known public designs, it is only because he was given a limited commission: turn a derelict dockyard into a public swimming park. He did so with characteristic style, linking the city to the sea with seawater pools and palm-strewn sundecks, and creating the city's favourite urban playground (completed in 1991).

Calatrava masterpiece The area brought to life by Parque Marítimo still needed a punctuation mark, and that commission fell to architect

Homenage a Santa Cruz, one of Manrique's distinctive wind sculptures, in Parque Marítimo (left); Manrique's swimming pool, complete with palm trees and sunbathing terraces (right)

Santiago Calatrava, who created the stunning white Auditorio (2003). Its semi-domed shape echoes the breaking surf below, and its soaring curves translate into perfect acoustics for performers inside. The Auditorio draws top names to a full slate of concerts, opera, dance and music events. It is home to the Orquestra Sinfonica de Tenerife.

Tiny fort In stark contrast to the pools and concert hall is the 1641 Castillo, black against the white of the Auditorio and the colourful turquoise and greens of the swimming park, and dwarfed by both. The little round fort, built of rough volcanic stone, sits almost completely surrounded by water. One of the best views of the Auditorio and the fort below it lapped by white surf is from the entrance to Calique 500, a lively outdoor nightspot at the end of the jetty.

THE BASICS

➕ K3

✉ Avenida de la Constitución

🕐 Daily 10–6

♿ Inexpensive

🚇 Short walk from central bus/Tranvia station

♿ Good

Auditorio

www.auditoriodetenerife.com

☎ 922 56 86 00

🕐 Box office Mon–Fri 10–3, Sat 10–2

Santa Cruz: Plaza de la Candelaria and Plaza de España

HIGHLIGHTS

● Cabildo Insular exterior and murals
● La Carta palace interior
● Monumento de los Caidos
● Cafés in Plaza de la Candelaria

TIPS

● Free evening concerts are often held in Plaza de la Candelaria.
● These plazas are the centre of action during Santa Cruz's pre-Lenten carnival festivities.

Santa Cruz is surprisingly urbane for an island capital, yet remains a delightfully approachable city. Its broad avenues further the sense of leisurely spaciousness created by the open sea that borders one entire side of the city.

Hub of the city's universe All activity seems to radiate from Plaza de España, much as the city's broad avenues themselves do. The Plaza is distinguished by the rationalist architecture of the Cabildo Insular building, seat of the island government, completed in 1940. Inside are murals by José Aguiar, an artist originally from La Gomera. Facing the Cabildo is the Monumento de los Caidos, commemorating those fallen in war. It was from this spot that Franco's manifesto was broadcast.

Monumento de los Caidos (left); outdoor cafés in Plaza de la Candelaria (middle and right)

Where everyone goes It's hard to tell where Plaza de España ends and Plaza de la Candelaria begins—the two seem to blend into one grand salon for the city. When festivals, concerts or just a warm Saturday evening brings people to Santa Cruz, it's here they gather and stroll. Overlooking Plaza de Candelaria is the façade of the 18th-century La Carta palace, now a bank. Step inside to see the real glory of this former noble mansion, which has been painstakingly restored. In the middle of the square is a baroque image of Nuestra Señora de la Candelaria, the island's patron. Unlike Plaza de España, around which traffic navigates, Plaza de la Candelaria is for pedestrians only, as are most of the streets that climb the gentle rise behind it. The plaza was once the entrance to the vanished Castillo San Cristóbal and now leads into the city's main shopping street, Calle de Castillo.

THE BASICS

✚ e3
✉ Santa Cruz
🍴 Several in Plaza de la Candelaria
🚃 Tranvia 'Fundación'
♿ Good
ℹ️ Plaza de España 1, tel 922 23 98 11 or 922 23 95 92; Oct–Jun Mon–Fri 8–6, Sat 9–1; Jul–Sep Mon–Fri 8–5, Sat 9–12

More to See

BASÍLICA DE NUESTRA SEÑORA DE CANDELARIA

www.candelaria.es

Local legend has it that before the Spanish arrived, a statue of the Virgin washed ashore and was worshipped by the Guanches. The Basilica is a shrine to the Virgin and is a major pilgrimage venue. The cave where the image was found is on the shore at the cliff.

➕ J4 ✉ Plaza Candelaria, Candelaria (off TF1) 🕓 Daily 7.30–1, 3–7.30 🚌 TITSA bus 120, 122 from Santa Cruz ♿ Few 🎟 Free

CASA DEL VINO LA BARANDA AND CASA DE LA MIEL

www.cabtfe.es/casa-vino
www.casadelamiel.com

Dedicated not only to wine-making but to rural life, the living museum has a bodega and wine-tasting room along with exhibits on the history and methods of wine production. The adjoining Casa de la Miel explains honey production. The 17th-century chapel ceiling is carved from Canarian pine.

➕ H2 ✉ Autopista General del Norte (km 21), El Sauzal (follow signs left from rotunda at TF5 La Baranda exit) ☎ 922 57 25 35. Casa de la Miel 922 56 27 11 🕓 Apr–Oct Tue 11.30–7.30; Nov–Mar Tue 10.30–6.30, Wed–Sat 10–9.30, Sun 11–6.30. Casa de la Miel May–Jul, Sep Mon–Thu 8.30–5, Fri 8.30–2.30, Sat 10–2; Oct–Apr Mon–Thu 8.30–2.30 🍴 Traditional island dishes (€€) 🚌 TITSA bus 101 ♿ None 🎟 Free

LA LAGUNA: MUSEO DE LA SCIENCIA Y EL COSMOS

www.museosdetenerife.org

The magic of science is brought alive through more than 100 interactive scientific experiments and a planetarium.

➕ J2 ✉ La Vía Láctea, La Laguna ☎ 922 31 52 65 🕓 Tue–Sun 9–7 🚋 Tranvia stop ♿ Fair–good 🎟 Inexpensive

MUSEO DE HISTORIA Y ANTROPOLOGIA DE TENERIFE: CASA DE CARTA

www.museosdetenerife.org

An early island mansion in an attractive town contains collections

Basílica de Nuestra Señora de Candelaria

View from Casa del Vino La Baranda

highlighting Tenerife culture and industry. Gardens grow indigenous plants and local crops, and the museum shows local costumes, lifestyles, foods and work.

⊞ H2 ⊠ Calle El Vino 44 (off TF16), Valle de Guerra ☎ 922 54 63 00 ④ Tue–Sun 9–7, last admission 6.30pm ☐ TITSA bus 051 ⚿ Call ahead 〽 Inexpensive, half price with TITSA multi-journey pass

PUNTA DEL HIDALGO

The only road into the Anaga peninsula's wild north coast ends at this attractive town of coloured houses, where hikers begin treks into the mountains. Drive along the coast on Camino el Costal de San Juaquinto to the *faro* (lighthouse), a striking modern shaft of narrow white columns overlooking natural rock pools and breaking surf. Behind, the sharp Anaga peaks line up like teeth. At a mirador at the end of TF13 there's a helpful tourist office.

⊞ J1 〽 Several along shore ☐ TITSA bus 105 ⚿ Few 〽 Free ℹ At end

of TF13, tel 922 15 78 32; Mon–Fri 9–3; Sat–Sun closed

SANTA CRUZ: IGLESIA DE SAN FRANCISCO

A triumph of baroque decorative art, the Franciscan church is all zthat remains of the monastery that filled the block. The entire wall of the high altar is covered in gilded carving, while either of the two ornate side altars and four chapels would be prized as the main altar of a smaller church. Painted wood panels cover the sanctuary ceiling, and the suspended pulpit is also painted.

⊞ d3 ⊠ Calle Villalba Hervas, Santa Cruz ④ Mon–Fri 9–1, 5.30–8 〽 Café in Plaza Principe (€) ⚿ None 〽 Free

SANTA CRUZ: MUSEO MUNICIPAL DE BELLAS ARTES

Surprising collection of Tenerife and Canarian artists—landscapes that record the island as it was, portraits that capture the character of both aristocrats and labourers.

Museo Municipal de Bellas Artes in Santa Cruz

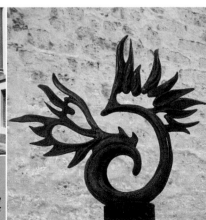

Decoration outside Iglesia de San Francisco, Santa Cruz

Collections include medal-winners from the great 1890 Exposition and contemporary works.

✚ d3 ✉ Calle Jose Murphy 12, Plaza del Principe, Santa Cruz ☎ 922 24 43 58 ⏰ Tue–Fri 10–8, Sat–Sun 10–3 🍴 Café in Plaza Principe (€) ♿ None 💵 Free

SANTA CRUZ: NUESTRA SEÑORA DE LA CONCEPCIÓN

Begun within a few years of the conquest, in 1502, the church holds the tomb of General Gutierrez, who defeated Nelson in 1797, and a British flag captured during the battle.

✚ d4 ✉ Plaza de la Iglesia, Santa Cruz ⏰ Daily 9–1, 4.30–8 🍴 Nearby on Calle Antonio Alfonso 🚌 Central bus/Tranvia station nearby ♿ Few 💵 Free

SANTA CRUZ: PARQUE GARCÍA SANABRIA

Fountains, reflecting pools, showy flowerbeds, contemporary sculptures and occasional festivals fill this beautiful green space in the heart of the city.

✚ c1–c2 ✉ Calle Méndez Nuñez, Santa Cruz 🍴 Café ♿ Very good 💵 Free

EL SAUZAL

The town drops in layers past the Church of San Pedro's low, round white dome, a reminder of the influence of many centuries of Moorish rule. Its pleasant plaza has views down into a garden and up to a perfectly shaped dragon tree. To find Mirador Garoñona follow signs to the right from the TF5 exit.

✚ H2 ✉ TF172 🍴 Restaurants line TF152 between El Sauzal and Tacaronte 🚌 TITSA bus 011, 101 ♿ None

TACARONTE

The church of Santo Cristo, which overlooks a wide plaza, has a much-venerated statue of Christ and a spectacular silver altar. The ceiling above is Mudejar and paintings are 17th-century baroque.

✚ H2 ✉ Tourist office TF16 ☎ 922 57 00 15 ⏰ Mon–Fri 9–1 🍴 Along TF152 between El Sauzal and Tacaronte 🚌 TITSA bus 101 ♿ None 💵 Free

The church of Nuestra Señora de la Concepción, Santa Cruz

Parque García Sanabria—an oasis in the heart of Santa Cruz

Leisurely City Streets, Santa Cruz

The compact central area, much of it closed to traffic, is a pleasure to explore on foot, with distinguished architecture and leafy parks.

DISTANCE: 2km (1.2 miles) **ALLOW:** 2 hours, with stops

START

PLAZA DE LA IGLESIA
d4 🚋 Tranvia 'Fundación'

END

PARQUE GARCÍA SANABRIA
c1 🚋 Rambla General Franco

① Begin in Plaza de la Iglesia, at Nuestra Señora de la Concepción church (▷ 42), begun in 1502.

② Cross the footbridge from the church to the impressive former hospital, now the Museo de la Naturaleza y el Hombre (▷ 34–35).

③ Leave Plaza de la Iglesia on Calle Candelaria, following the Tranvia tracks briefly to the right and turning left on Calle General Gutiérrez into Plaza de España. On your right is the 1940 rationalist-style Cabildo Insular building; ahead is the Monumento de los Caídos, commemorating war dead.

④ Go left into adjoining Plaza de la Candelaria, past the baroque statue of Nuestra Señora de Candelaria. Look into the 18th-century La Carta Palace, now a bank.

⑧ Follow Calle Pilar uphill to the right, crossing Calle Méndez Nuñez into Parque García Sanabria (▷ 42).

⑦ After stopping at the Museo Municipal de Bellas Artes, climb the steps into Plaza del Principe and continue to its other side. Follow the short street ahead into a small star-shaped plaza. The ornate pink building ahead was a tobacco factory.

⑥ Turn left onto Calle Verde into Plaza San Francisco. Above is Iglesia de San Francisco, one of the island's loveliest baroque churchs (▷ 41). Go left on leaving the church, and left again at the end of the park.

⑤ Follow the plaza uphill onto Calle de Castillo, Santa Cruz's main shopping street. Go right on Calle Valentin Sanz and right again on Calle Bethencourt Alfonso.

THE NORTH

WALK

43

In the Anaga Mountains

Choose a sunny day for this spectacular drive along the ridge that connects the jagged peaks of the Anaga Mountains.

DISTANCE: 52km (32 miles) **ALLOW:** 4 hours, with stops

START

CRUZ DEL CARMEN
✚ K2

1 After enjoying the views and learning about the human and natural history of the mountains at Cruz del Carmen visitor centre, head east (right) on TF12.

2 Detour right to Pico del Inglés, on a shoulder of the park's highest peak, Mount Taborno, for spectacular views from the mirador.

3 Return to TF12 and continue through tiny Casas de la Cumbre to the ridge's sharpest and narrowest point, at Cruz de Taganana, where the road narrows to one lane with views down to the sea on both sides.

4 After the road begins to descend, turn left on TF134, signposted Taganana. Be prepared for breathtaking views (and turns) as the road drops sharply to the sea.

END

SAN ANDRÉS
✚ L2

8 Return to TF12, turning left to descend through Barranco de las Huertas to tree-shaded San Andrés and the sea.

7 Shortly beyond, past beaches popular with surfers, the road climbs to Benijo, a cluster of houses and Restaurant Mirador (€–€€), hanging far above a long sand beach that is accessed by a steep path.

6 Continue down to the shore, where a cluster of restaurants at Roque de las Bodegas faces a series of sandy beaches. The name is a reminder that Taganana was once Tenerife's major wine export port.

5 At Taganana a car park on the right allows visitors to walk into the village to see traditional old houses and the church, which has an especially fine triptych.

Shopping

CASA DEL REGALO
www.casa-balcones.com
In case you missed the chance to buy colourful embroidered clothing and household linens at the Casa de los Balcones in La Orotava, there's a branch in the capital, too. There are frequent demonstrations of lace-making.
🕂 d3 ✉ Calle Castillo 30, Santa Cruz ☎ 922 24 57 34 🕐 Mon–Sat 10–8

LES CHAMPS
Stylish women's clothing and urban accessories for the fashion-conscious.
🕂 d2 ✉ Calle El Pilar 8, Santa Cruz 🕐 Mon–Sat 10–9

EL CORTE INGLÉS
www.elcorteingles.es
Spain's favourite department store. The lower floor is a gourmet shop, good for ready-to-eat meals and food gifts to take home, the upper floors stock clothing, accessories, gifts, cosmetics and kitchen gear.
🕂 c5 ✉ Avenida Tres de Mayo 7, Santa Cruz ☎ 922 84 94 00 🕐 Mon–Sat 10–8 🚌 Near central bus/Tranvia station

GALIANA
Top names in continental women's fashions—Rinascimento, Labanda, Andres Sarda—in a serene, unhurried setting.
🕂 J2 ✉ Calle Heraclio Sanchez 23, La Laguna ☎ 922 25 12 07 🕐 Mon–Fri 9–1, 5–8, Sat 9–1

LA ISLA LIBROS
www.laislalibros.com
Need a Spanish–English dictionary or a book to help you brush up on school-day Spanish? La Isla has these, as well as travel guides and a selection of titles in English.
🕂 c3 ✉ Calle Robayna 2, Santa Cruz ☎ 922 28 54 81 🕐 Daily 🚋 Tranvia 'Guimera'

MERCADILLO DEL AGRICULTOR Y ARTESANO
A superior farmers' market with 33 booths selling vegetables, fruit, local cheeses, wines, baskets, handicrafts and even salted fish.
🕂 J2 ✉ Calle Asuncionistas 6, Tegueste ☎ 922 54 23 05 🕐 Sat, Sun and holidays 8.30–2 🚌 TITSA bus 051, 105 ♿ Good

NATURA
Organic and natural fabrics, timeless styles and earth-tone colour

schemes can all be found here for casual style-conscious travellers. Smart backpacks and other practical accessories make this a refreshing stop for those who don't fancy the excesses of high fashion.
🕂 d2 ✉ Calle El Pilar 16, Santa Cruz ☎ 922 28 81 80 🕐 Mon–Sat 10–8.30

THE OUTLET
You may have met this chain elsewhere in Spain or perhaps in Italy, with phenomenal discounts on all the big brand names such as Diesel, Armani, Versace, Hugo Boss and Guru.
🕂 c3 ✉ Calle Suarez Guerra 21–23, Santa Cruz ☎ 922 29 94 12 🕐 Mon–Sat 10–8

ROCCO
High-fashion accessories for men and women, from designer hats and sunglasses to the latest in handbags.
🕂 b5 (fold-out map) ✉ Centro Comercial, Calle Tres de Mayo, Santa Cruz ☎ 922 53 57 20 🕐 Mon–Sat 10–8, Sun 10–2

ZEBINA EXQUISITECES
Wine and locally produced gourmet food products, including a large selection of goodies for unwinding after a hard day's sightseeing.
🕂 J2 ✉ Calle Herradores 66, La Laguna ☎ 922 57 00 39 🕐 Mon–Fri 9–1.15, 5–10.15, Sat 9–2

Entertainment and Activities

ARCO PUB

Enjoy a brightly coloured cocktail while listening to a live band—rock, indie or jazz.

➕ K2 ✉ Avenida Anaga 31, Santa Cruz ⏰ Daily until late

AUDITORIO

www.auditoriodetenerife.com
The stunning auditorium (▷ 36–37) by Santiago Calatrava is the home of the Orquestra Sinfonica de Tenerife, and also hosts major European orchestras.

➕ K3 ✉ Avenida de la Constitución, Santa Cruz ☎ 902 31 73 27 ⏰ Box office Mon–Fri 10–3, 5–7, Sat 10–2 🍴 On plaza 🚌 Central bus/Tranvia station ♿ Good

BODEGAS MONJE

www.bodegasmonje.com
The Monje family has been making wine here since 1750. Visitors see the vineyards, enjoy tastings and, with advance notice, can arrange private tours. A wine garden celebrates not only the vineyard but the ecological diversity of the island.

➕ H2 ✉ Camino Cruz Leandro, 36, El Sauzal ☎ 922 58 50 27 ⏰ Mon–Fri 10–7, Sat 10–2 🚌 TITSA bus 101

DREAMS TENERIFE

www.dreamstenerife.com
Overlooking Parque Marítimo, Las Cascadas packs the house out for big international names, and is definitely thought of as the hottest disco on the island.

➕ K3 ✉ Las Cascadas, Avenida de la Constitución 5, Santa Cruz ☎ 922 21 65 48 ⏰ Mon–Thu 8.30pm–2am, Fri–Sat 8.30pm–2.30am 🚌 Central bus/Tranvia station

HEAVEN TENERIFE

Traditional pub with 70s, 80s and 90s music.

➕ a2 (fold-out map) ✉ Calle General Goded 24, Santa Cruz ⏰ Fri–Sat and holidays 11pm–4am 🚌 Tranvia 'La Paz'

HIKING IN THE ANAGA MOUNTAINS

Punta del Hidalgo (▷ 41) is the most popular starting point for hikes into the Anaga Mountains. Begin at the tourist office, where you'll find the most complete selection of annotated maps and brochures describing the trails in detail. Hike from there or from the trailhead at the end of the Camino el Costal de San Juaquinto, past the lighthouse.

➕ J1 🍴 Several along shore 🚌 TITSA bus 105 ℹ End of TF13, tel 922 15 78 32; Mon–Fri 9–3

PIRATA BRASILEIRO

Club featuring the many influences of black and Hispanic music that define the Brazilian genre.

➕ J2 ✉ Calle Antonio Glez 5, La Laguna ⏰ Daily 9pm–3am 🚌 Tranvia 'Trinidad'

PRIMI

A popular restaurant and bar that serves drinks from 3pm, and offers plenty of live music of all styles.

➕ Off map ✉ Avenida de la Constitución, Santa Cruz ☎ 922 20 94 25 ⏰ Mon–Sat 1–4, 8.30–midnight 🚌 Central bus station

TEATRO GUIMERÁ

www.teatroguimera.es
The place to go for culture—plays, classical music and ballet.

➕ d3 ✉ Plaza Isla de la Madera, Santa Cruz ☎ 902 33 33 38 ⏰ Scheduled performances

TEATRO LEAL

La Laguna's venue for concerts and performance, a grand turn-of-the-20th-century theatre.

➕ J2 ✉ Calle Obispo Rey Redondo, La Laguna ☎ 922 60 11 00 ⏰ Scheduled performances 🚌 Tranvia 'Trinidad'

LA NORIA 1

The place to go at night in Santa Cruz is Calle de la Noria, though you won't find that name on a map or street sign. But ask for it by its proper name—Calle Antonio Domínguez Alfonso—and you might only get a shrug and a blank look. 'La Noria' is where the evening action is, a short wide street lined with restaurants and cafés spilling out onto the pavement. At night, music fills the air and people fill the street.

Restaurants

PRICES

Prices are approximate, based on a three-course meal for one person.

€€€	over €25
€€	€15–€25
€	under €15

BODEGA SAN SEBASTIÁN €€–€€€

Traditional dining in a wine cellar atmosphere, with a wide selection of wines and a tasting room.
➕ d4 ✉ Calle de San Sebastián, Santa Cruz, near the market ☎ 922 21 68 53 🕐 Lunch, dinner 🚊 Tranvia 'Guimera'

BULAN €–€€

In an old house amid a solid line of cafés and restaurants, Bulan has a bar on the patio, street tables and small rooms inside. Canarian comfort food with a few contemporary touches is served amid rustic furniture and contemporary paintings. There's music most Saturday nights.
➕ d4 ✉ Calle Antonio Domínguez Alfonso (La Noria) 35, Santa Cruz ☎ 922 27 41 16 🕐 Daily lunch, dinner

CAFÉ CAPRICCIO €

This café at Mirador Garañona is at the end of a stone-paved promenade that drops down through trees and steep terraced flower gardens, revealing vertiginous views to the deep blue sea below. The ice cream

is as good as the view.
➕ H2 ✉ Mirador Garañona, Rondo El Sauzalito, El Sauzal 🕐 Thu–Mon 11–10 🚌 TITSA bus 101

IL CAFFE DI ROMA €

The old-fashioned ornate café in a belle epoque tobacco factory dishes up outstanding *gelati* in unusual flavours, along with a staggering variety of coffees from all over the world.
➕ d3 ✉ Calle El Pilar 3, Santa Cruz ☎ 922 27 20 31 🕐 Daily 8am–midnight (till 1am Sat–Sun)

CASA TITA €–€€

Popular local restaurant serving traditional dishes, on the main street of the upper town.
➕ J1 ✉ Carreterra General Punta del Hidalgo (TF13), Punta del Hidalgo ☎ 922 15 66 22 🕐 Daily lunch, dinner 🚌 TITSA bus 105

LA NORIA 2

Calle de Noria–Calle Antonio Domínguez Alfonso, to be correct–may be one of Santa Cruz's premier nightlife zones, but don't overlook it for dining and cafés as well. On a weekend afternoon, the place is just as busy, with the tables filled with patrons of all ages; for families it's a good traffic-free place to meet friends while children play in the space between the facing rows of tables.

LA CASETA €–€€

Traditional menu of local seafood and sea views.
➕ J1 ✉ Avenida Maritima 1, Punta del Hidalgo ☎ 922 15 66 32 🕐 Daily lunch, dinner 🚌 TITSA bus 105

LA CAZUELA €€

An attractive restaurant serving tasty, creative dishes based on Basque cuisine, but with Canarian overtones.
➕ b2 (fold-out map) ✉ Calle Robayna 34, Santa Cruz ☎ 922 27 23 00 🕐 Mon–Sat 1.30–4, 8–midnight

LOS CHURRITOS CASA FERNANDO €–€€

Quick and easy dining in San Andrés, close to Las Teresitas beach. Famed for their *churros de pescado* (fried fish sticks).
➕ L2 ✉ Calle El Dique, San Andrés 🕐 Mon–Fri lunch and dinner 🚌 TITSA bus 245, 246, 910

COFRADIA DE PESCADORES €–€€

The name suggests the menu; specialties of the house are fish and seafood, fresh from the boats in the pretty little fishing harbour below.
➕ J1 ✉ La Hoya Abajo, Punta del Hidalgo ☎ 922 15 69 54 🕐 Tue–Sun lunch, dinner 🚌 TITSA bus 105

DON PELAYO €€–€€€

A chance to savour the taste of Spain's Asturias region, perhaps with

THE NORTH | **RESTAURANTS**

fabada Asturiana (bean stew) or a steak fillet with Cabrales cheese sauce.
➕ a3 (fold-out map)
✉ Calle Benavides 30, Santa Cruz ☎ 922 27 11 59
🕐 Daily 1–4.30, 8–1

HELADERÍA LA FLOR DE ALICANTE €

Famed for the ice creams and pastries they have been making for 60 years, this *heladeria* is in a residential neighbourhood near Sanabria Park.
➕ d2 ✉ Calle La Rosa 29, Santa Cruz ☎ 922 28 34 61
🕐 Daily 8–8

LA HIERBITA €–€€

www.lahierbita.com
A favourite with the locals for the atmosphere, good food and friendly service; look out for the *carne fiesta* which is excellent.
➕ d3 ✉ Calle El Clavel 19, Santa Cruz ☎ 922 24 46 17
🕐 Mon–Sat lunch, dinner

MARTÍNEZ

www.restaurantemartinez.com
Well loved local restaurant with a large menu of fish and meats, including beef, veal, goat and rabbit; tasty *carne fiesta* is often a special.
➕ H2 ✉ Carretera General del Norte 119, El Sauzal
☎ 922 56 40 44 🕐 Thu–Tue 9.30–4, Fri 9.30–4, 7–11
🚌 TITSA bus 101

OH LA LÁ €

A good place for a quick *bocadillo* (a sandwich, usually of ham and/or cheese) or snack.

Fresh croissants, breads, baguettes with a great selection of fillings.
➕ J2 ✉ Calle Obisbo Rey Redondo (La Carrera), La Laguna ☎ 922 25 82 19
🕐 Daily 9am–10pm

OH LA LÁ €

Look here for a quick sandwich on fresh croissants, breads or baguettes, on the street opposite the port. A good choice for breakfast, and much better value than the cafés around the corner on the shopping streets.
➕ e2 ✉ Calle La Marina, Santa Cruz ☎ 922 24 28 24
🕐 Daily 9am–10pm

RESTAURANTE-CAFETERIA OLYMPO €

The menu has everything from hamburgers to calamares and pork loin, plus a number of Galician specialties with a good selection of Spanish *tortillas* (omelettes).
➕ d3 ✉ Plaza de La Candelaria 1, Santa Cruz
☎ 922 24 17 38 🕐 Lunch, dinner

RESTAURANTE SANCHEZ €–€€

Loved by locals for its traditional Canarian cuisine, Sanchez is one of several restaurants that bring diners to Punta del Hidalgo.
➕ J1 ✉ Carretera General Punta del Hidalgo (TF13), Punta del Hidalgo ☎ 922 15 66 08 🕐 Daily lunch, dinner
🚌 TITSA bus 105

TABERNA RAMON €–€€

Always filled with locals—usually a good sign—this taverna is a good place to sample typical Canarian specialties in either small tapas-sized or full servings.
➕ a2 (fold-out map)
✉ Rambla General Franco 56 (Plaza de Toros), Santa Cruz
☎ 922 24 13 67 🕐 Mon–Sat lunch, dinner 🚋 Tranvia 'La Paz'

TASCA SÁFRON Y EL PORRÓN €–€€

If eating light sounds good for you, then stop here for Andalucian tapas. The baby shrimp in garlic and olive oil are outstanding.
➕ d4 ✉ Calle La Noria 36, Santa Cruz ☎ 629 45 14 05
🕐 Daily lunch, dinner

CANARIAN FOODS

Carne fiesta: literally 'holiday meat', this is a savoury dish of meat braised until it is fork-tender.

Gofio: possibly the most typical Canarian specialty, this blend of roasted barley, maize and/or wheat has been eaten here since precolonial times. Today it's most often seen in puddings, combined with almonds and dried fruits, especially figs.

Potaje de berros: watercress soup.

The West

El Teide dominates this central part of the
island, dropping off only slightly to the
long spine of the Cumbre Dorsal. These
dramatic mountains form the backdrop for
the coastal resorts to the north and for the
gracious old town of La Orotava, which lies
partway up El Teide's northern slope.

Iglesia San Francisco,
Jardín Acuático Risco Bello,
Jardín Botánico,
Jardín Tauro,
Lago Martiánez,
Museo Arqueológico,
Nuestra Señora de la Pena de Francia,
PUERTO DE LA CRUZ
Playa Jardín
Loro Parque

Punta de Barranco
Hondo

TF-5

La Victoria
de Acentejo

29

TF-217

Santa Ursula

31

San Antonio

El Esquilón

Cuesta de la Villa

32

F-5

San Vicente

El Toscal

33

Oasis
del Valle

TF-5

1205
Montaña
Micheque

TF-24

Icod el
Alto

San Agustín

TF-315

34

TF-5

35

36

**Pueblo
Chico**

San
Miguel

La Orotava
Jardines Marquesado de la Quinta Roja,
Museo de Cerámica,
Nuestra Señora de la Concepción

TF-342

Los
Realejos

Cruz
Santa

TF-324

Camino
de Chasna

TF-21

1958
Joco

TF-523

La Ferruja

TF-326

Benijos

Aguamansa

Cumbre Dorsal

1217
Risco de las
Palmas

Vergara

La Calera

Guamasa

TF-21

Quiquira

Arafo

La Dahesa

TF-525

2111
Montaña Negra

TF-24

2269
Igueque

Agua

Parque
Nacional
del Teide

2222
Montaña de
los Gomillos

Las Cañadas
del Teide

2313
Los Mallorquines

2406
Abreo

1407
Montaña
de Amorin

Marrero
La Medida

TF-21

2748
Blanca

2305
Montaña Colmenas

La Rosa

El Escobona

TF-28

2250
Montaña de
la Cruz

2101
Montaña
de la Angostura

Fuente
Nueva

TF-532

Fasnia

2236

2281
Montaña
do Palo

1826
Los Albarderos

Chajaña

La Zarza

2712
Guajara

El Bueno

La Sombrera

Lomo
Oliva

TF-620

Cruz del
Roque

Cañadas

Río

1883
Montaña
Bermeja

1232
Risco Bermejo

TF-534

Arico Viejo

1835

Punta
de Honduras

Las Eras

TF-1

Punta
de la Ternera
Poris de
Abona

F

G

H

Acantilados de los Gigantes

TOP 25

The resort of Puerto de Santiago (left); boats at Los Gigantes harbour (right)

The mountains of the Teno Massif that make up western Tenerife end abruptly, plunging more than 600m (1,968ft) into the sea. The sheer cliff face is one of Tenerife's most spectacular sights.

Good beaches So vertical and so formidable is this 20km (12.5-mile) of untouched wilderness that it stops the coastal road, and the cliffs (aptly named Los Gigantes) are only glimpsed from *miradors* on the twisting road that descends to Puerto de Santiago and Los Gigantes village. Playa Santiago is a mix of old town and new, with a small beach of black sand and volcanic rock that has been sea-worn into natural arches. One of the island's nicest natural beaches, Playa de la Arena, is popular with young families and couples, and the broad sandy beach is protected by arms of volcanic rock and backed by a pleasant park of palms and flowers.

Best by boat The way to see Los Gigantes and to appreciate their height and grandeur is from a boat, and the trip is usually combined with watching the whales and dolphins that feed in these rich waters. *Nashira Uno*, a stable excursion ship with glass floor panels, makes one- and two-hour trips, and a three-hour trip that includes swimming and lunch at Masca Bay. Cruises on the sailing ketch *Flipper Uno* include swimming and a paella feast at Masca Bay. The smaller *Gladiator U* makes more frequent shorter cruises from Los Gigantes Harbour and operates a water taxi to remote Masca beach.

Cumbre Dorsal

El Teide looms ahead (left); the view to the northeast from Montana Grande (right)

You can drive along the ridge that divides the island, with far-reaching views of the south coast on one side, and then the Orotava valley and the sea off the north coast on the other.

Tenerife's spine The TF24 highway leaves the TF21 at El Portillo, near the National Park visitor centre, and traverses a fairly level route along the top of the ridge. Trails lead off through this wild open terrain, but be aware that clouds can quickly veil this shoulder of Spain's highest peak. The plateau's rocky landscape is clearly volcanic, and stops at viewing points give details of its geology.

Learning about volcanos The signs (in English) explain how the varied rocks and landscapes formed. Fantastical rock formations were carved out of the sandstone by high winds, and at La Tarta, where the road makes a hairpin turn, there is an especially dramatic eroded formation. The white layers of pumice blew from the Las Cañadas eruption, which hurled debris 20km (12 miles) into the air, while the dark red and black stripes are from nearer eruptions that blew only 1km (0.5 miles) high and fell directly down.

Stellar views The TF514 leads 1.5km (1 mile) to an observatory. The road adds different perspectives of Teide's entire cone rising above a vast bowl, in a notch between Montaña de Cerrillal and Montaña de Abreo. While no trees grow in this terrain, heather and broom bloom beside the road, and wildflowers provide splatters of colour.

THE BASICS

✚ G4–H4

✉ TF24

🍴 At El Portillo (€–€€)

🚌 No buses along TF24. Hikers take TITSA bus 342 or 348 to El Portillo

♿ Few

HIGHLIGHTS

● Views to north and south coasts
● Rock formations at La Tarta
● Road to observatory

Drago Milenario and Icod de los Vinos

Dragon trees are the botanical mascot of Tenerife, and almost every town has at least one. But Icod has the grandfather of them all, the largest and oldest known, claimed to be 1,000 years old.

A pleasant plaza Even without its famous tree (whose age may have lengthened a few centuries in legend), this attractive wine town would be worth visiting. Narrow streets climb the hill between fine old homes, and the central plaza is a cosy spot shaded by big trees of its own. The slightest excuse for a festival decks its streets and plaza with colourful banners, and locals enjoy strolling there as much as visitors do. On Thursday and Saturday, a few local craftsmen set up tables, including glass artist Santini (at other times you can see his work at Calle Real 90).

Clockwise from left: Attractive houses line the streets of Icod de los Vinos; the Drago Milenario; Papilio glaucus butterfly in the Mariposario (Butterfly Garden) next to the Parque del Drago; banana plantations around Icod; La Casa del Drago shop

The big tree But Icod's fame rests on the tree, *Dracaena draco*, a species that has changed little since dinosaurs nibbled it. Its curiously bundled trunk and compactly branching top give it a distinctive look, but it is the resin, which turns deep red on contact with air, that assured its place in local legend. The aboriginal guanches are said to have revered it, but all that's known for certain is that they used the strange resin in embalming.

Church treasure The entrance to the garden surrounding the tree is down a side street beyond Plaza Constitución, where the church of San Marcos is well worth visiting for its silver and gold altar and blend of Mudejar, baroque and gothic elements. In its little museum (Mon–Fri 9.30–6, Sat 9.30–2) is one of the finest silver filigree crosses in Spain.

THE BASICS

✚ D4
🍴 Cafés in plaza (€)
🚌 TITSA buses 107, 108, 325
♿ None
🎟 Drago Park moderate (tickets at tourism kiosk below plaza)
ℹ Calle San Sebastian 6, tel 922 81 21 23; Mon–Fri 9–1, 3–7, Sat 10–1

HIGHLIGHTS

● Natural lava swimming pools
● Iglesia Santa Ana
● Convento de San Francisco
● Castillo de San Miguel
● Parque de la Puerta de Terra

TIP

● In the Convent of San Francisco there's a map showing the exact path of the lava, still traceable as you explore today.

It may have taken nearly three centuries, but clever Garachico has snatched a victory from the disastrous volcanic eruption that destroyed its harbour. Today in the black lava a beautiful recreation area enhances natural swimming pools.

Lava pools Seawater fills natural pools in the lava, where it flowed into the sea in 1706, and around them are flattened places to sunbathe. The pools are different depths, ranging from places shallow enough for children to paddle to a long deep channel for diving. A restaurant is hidden under the street, its terrace overlooking pools. Although not designed by César Manrique, it was certainly inspired by his work. Overlooking one end is little Castillo de San Miguel, built to defend the town from pirates, and one of the

few survivors of the eruption. Inside is a collection of fossils, and stairs to the ramparts.

In the Old Town A five-minute walk inland leads to a leafy little sunken park. The stone 'Puerta de Tierra' (Land Gate) at its centre, now well below street level, is all that remains of what was once Tenerife's most prosperous port. Its main exports were for wine, sugar and leather and in the garden above is a well-preserved old wine press. Plaza de Arriba, another tree-shaded park, is flanked by Iglesia Santa Ana and the Convento de San Francisco, whose grand stone staircase has an elaborate Mudejar ceiling. The adjoining church of Nuestra Señora de los Angeles also has a fine ceiling. Little wine bars and restaurants on side streets, some in fine old balconied mansions, invite lingering in the appealing town.

THE BASICS

+ D4
¶ Several
🚌 TITSA buses 107, 363
& Few
ℹ Esteban del Ponte 5, tel 922 13 34 61; Mon–Thu 10–7, Fri 10–2, 3–7, Sat–Sun 10–1

Loro Parque

Parrot, Loro Parque (left); the Thai Village, Loro Parque's main buildings (right)

THE BASICS

www.loroparque.com

🔲 F3

✉ Avenida Loro Parque, Puerto de la Cruz

☎ 922 37 38 41

🕐 Daily 8.30–6.45 (last admission at 4)

🍴 On site (€–€€)

🚌 Free Express road train daily every 20 mins from Puerto de la Cruz waterfront near Ermita San Telmo

♿ Few–good

💲 Very expensive

HIGHLIGHTS

● Orca Ocean
● Loro Show
● Kinderlandia
● Planet Penguin
● Natura Vision Show

DID YOU KNOW?

● Orca Ocean contains 22 million litres of sea water.
● Loro Parque contains more than 7,000 palm trees.
● The park started as a showplace for parrots.

Whales, dolphins, tigers, gorillas, parrots and alligators live in their own natural environments at Spain's most popular zoo, where 4,000 creatures represent more than 350 different species.

See sea creatures Loro Parque joins zoo, marine park and gardens in one place. Regularly scheduled shows in the specially built Orca Ocean let visitors get up close to see these sleek black and white sea mammals. Close by, in a separate lake, the largest pod of dolphins in Europe perform amazing tricks, while a short distance away sea lions have their chance at glory. There is even an aquarium where sharks and other sea creatures eye passing tourists, up close, but safely.

Plenty of penguins Sea and land blend at Planet Penguin, where an enormous man-made iceberg cools the largest group of penguins in captivity. But they are not the only exotic birds here. A colony of ungainly pelicans fishes for lunch in its own pond, while elsewhere a big flock of brightly coloured macaws squawk about their jungle hide-away. Farther on, pink flamingoes stalk about.

Natural surroundings The animals here live in a naturalized lush park especially designed to resemble their natural habitats, not only a good living environment for the animals, but a more realistic experience for visitors. In the primate collection, monkeys, gorillas, marmosets and chimps are cousins that everyone loves to watch, and cat-lovers can find lions, tigers and even rare jaguars.

Puerto de la Cruz: Lago Martiánez

The fishing village of Puerto de la Cruz had coarse black volcanic lava when Lanzarote artist and architect César Manrique was commissioned to create a glamorous resort here.

Manrique's vision Manrique is known throughout the islands for his love of their terrain and ecology. While recognizing the potential benefit of tourism for the islanders, he also believed that to preserve the beauty and character of the islands it was necessary to work with the land, not against it. His dream for the Canary Islands' future was of a place filled with artistic and architectural attractions.

Texture and colour Manrique took advantage of the stark black and coarse texture of the lava, contrasting it with smooth white surfaces and highlighting the swimming and wading pools with bright turquoise shades borrowed from the surrounding sea. Attractive walkways and bridges wind through the rough black rock, connecting seven ponds of various sizes. The largest is Lago Martiánez itself, more than 15,000sq m (160,000sq ft) with an island in its centre. An open-air whirlpool pool is accented with lighting effects. Palm trees and gardens soften the dramatic contrasts and Manrique's trademark whimsical sculptures add the finishing touch. Locals mix with visitors at Lago Martiánez, for sunbathing, swimming, dining, drinking and just hanging out. Facilities include sunbeds, bars, restaurants and ice cream vendors. Puerto Cruz's casino is hidden under the island in the middle of the lake.

THE BASICS

* F3
* Avenida de Colon, Puerto de la Cruz
* 922 38 59 55
* May–Sep daily 10–7; Oct–Apr daily 10–6
* Plentiful
* TITSA bus 381, 382
* Few
* Moderate (includes sunbed)

DID YOU KNOW?

● César Manrique created seven major attractions, a hotel complex, several restaurants and numerous 'wind toys' for his native island of Lanzarote.
● Manrique designed his own home and an entire auditorium inside *jameos*— long caves and sinkholes created by fast-cooling lava.

Puerto de la Cruz: Jardín Acuático Risco Bello

TOP 25

The Risco Bello garden is a harmonious blend of plants and architectural features

THE BASICS

- F3
- ✉ Carretera Taoro 15, Puerto de la Cruz
- 🕐 Daily 9.30–6
- 🍴 Tea, coffee and pastries served on the lawn and in bar inside the villa (€)
- 🚌 TITSA buses 101, 103
- ♿ None
- 💰 Moderate

HIGHLIGHTS

- The upper lily pond
- The terracotta jug 'waterfall'
- Tea and cakes on the lawn

There is no hint of what lies below as visitors cross the well-kept lawn dotted with tea tables set among the fragrant flowering shrubs, and step into this modern version of the Hanging Gardens of Babylon.

A green love story Created 40 years ago by the present owner's Belgian father for her mother but only opened to the public in 2004, Risco Bello (literally 'beautiful hillside') is a water garden built in an almost vertical landscape. Level after level of pools, ponds, fountains, flower beds and trees unfold, each disclosed by a pathway or set of stairs almost hidden in the profusion of 600 plant varieties. Surprises are everywhere—overflowing terracotta jugs form fountains and create waterfalls, stepping stones lead across a lily pond to disclose a garden walk, a grape arbour hides behind a row of fruit trees, and at the very bottom a red bridge arches over a pond lined with beach-worn stones, with benches in a shaded nook for admiring the scene.

An artist's eye The design of the gardens is so brilliant that each few steps lead to a perfect frame—a window in a grotto, a vine-draped arbour, an artfully placed tree, an aerial perspective from a bridge—for viewing another scene. Shrubs are placed to hide the buildings below, but kept low enough to disclose the mountainside studded with the villas of Orotava, which form the backdrop. The city that surrounds the gardens seems to disappear.

Puerto de la Cruz: Jardín Botánico

HIGHLIGHTS

- *Ficus* at entrance used as a planter for orchids
- Giant banyan tree
- Coral trees covered with bright red blossoms
- *Ficus macrophylla* from Lord Howe Island

TIP

- Keep an eye on where the groundsmen are watering—or have just watered—unless you welcome a sudden shower.

Cool, moist and shaded, smelling of damp earth and opening blossoms, this Eden of exotic plants is one of the city's most popular non-beach attractions, though it was intended for botanic purposes, not recreation.

Home away for plants In the late 1800s, as botanic explorers returned from Spain's far-flung empire with rare exotic plants, King Charles III saw the need to acclimatize plants if they were to thrive in European gardens. The moderate and protected climate of Tenerife's northern shore proved the perfect spot, proven by such successes as the gargantuan *Ficus* from Lord Howe Island (off the east coast of Australia) that towers over one entire section, its draping branches intertangled into a forest of new trunks.

Clockwise from top left: Strelitzia, or bird of paradise bloom; ornamental water lily pond; variegated foliage; white peace lilies

Something for everyone Avid gardeners read the labels and marvel at the giant specimens of familiar garden and house plants—each stem of a tangled and sprawling cut-leaf philodendron is thicker than a man's arm, and one gardenia plant has grown here to the size of an apple tree, testimony to the benign climate here. Others simply stroll or sit on the benches inhaling the heady scents of tropical flowers and enjoying the cool serenity. Children are fascinated to find fruits that at home they know only from the greengrocer growing on trees. At the centre of the garden, water lilies, their leaves like platters with upturned rims, float in a pond. Although the gardens are designed with an eye to practicality, beauty is clearly also a priority, with beds neatly edged in rows of low-growing plants, such as sanseveria, to form miniature natural fences.

THE BASICS

➕ F3
✉ Calle Retama 2, Puerto de la Cruz
☎ 922 38 35 72, 922 38 94 64
🕓 Apr–Sep daily 9–7, Oct–Mar daily 9–6
🍴 Opposite entrance (€–€€)
🚌 TITSA bus 101, 345, 348 to Orotava
♿ Few
💶 Inexpensive

Shopping for Crafts in La Orotava

HIGHLIGHTS

● Casa de los Balcones
● Casa Lercaro
● Nuestra Señora de la Concepción
● Museo de Artesanía Iberoamerica

TIPS

● Don't come on a Sunday, when nearly everything is closed.
● The Jardínes Marquesado de la Quinta Roja (▷ 68) make a good finish to a day of exploring genteel Orotava.

Depending on perspective, craft shopping is a good way to see La Orotava's abundant fine colonial buildings. Or touring its major sites could be an excuse to shop for the crafts that are also its hallmark.

Colonial architecture Calle San Francisco is lined with fine old mansions. Begin at Casa de los Balcones, a 1632 noble home with traditional carved wooden balconies, now a centre for Tenerife needle arts, demonstrated in the courtyard overlooked by more wooden balconies. Upstairs a small museum shows 17th-century noble family life. Opposite in another fine mansion are more showrooms.

Wines and crafts The street drops past the Dias Flores and Ponte family mansions. The latter

Clockwise from far left: Pots for sale in Casa de los Balcones; needlewoman in traditional dress, Casa del Turista; work in progress in Casa Torrehermosa; Jardínes Marquesado de la Quinta Roja; lace maker at work; richly embroidered waistcoat, Casa de los Balcones

houses Casa Lercaro, a place to enjoy local wines and cheeses in the bodega, pause for a bite in the patio or shop for quality decorator items, many crafted locally (tel 922 32 62 04; shop open Mon–Sat 10–8, bodega to midnight).

Street of mansions Below to the right is Nuestra Señora de la Concepcion (▷ 69), and the street leading from its portal ends at Calle Tomas Zerolo, lined with more mansions. Follow it left past six of these before reaching the beautiful former convent of Santo Domingo, now the Museo de Artesanía Iberoamerica, displaying handicrafts from Latin America and Spain (tel 922 32 17 46; open Mon 9–3, Tue–Fri 9–5, Sat 9–1). Opposite, yet another mansion contains Artenerife Casa Torrehermosa, an *artesania* selling exceptional local crafts (tel 922 32 22 85).

THE BASICS

www.villadelaorotava.org

🔲 G4

🍴 Several

🚌 TITSA buses 101, 107, 108, 345, 347

🅸 Calle Calvario 4, tel 922 32 30 41; Mon–Fri 8.30–6

Casa de los Balcones

www.casa-balcones.com

✉ Calle San Francisco 3–4

☎ 922 33 06 29

🕐 Mon–Fri 8.30–6.30, Sat 8.30–5 🔳 Free; museum inexpensive

El Teide

HIGHLIGHTS

● Roques de García
● Teleférico cable car
● Zapatilla de Reiña arch

TIPS

● Buses are not well timed for park visiting except as a drive-through.
● Walk the trail through the botanic garden at El Portillo for views and rare plants.
● If you want to hike to the summit, you will need to obtain a permit in advance (tel 922 29 01 29).

If Spain's highest peak, El Teide, seems impressive, imagine the size of the volcanic cone that left this 17km (10.5-mile) crater when its top slid into the sea. Enter it to find lunar landscapes, dramatic rock formations and flora unknown elsewhere.

Still simmering The island's main north–south road, TF21, crosses the rim of Teide's crater at two places, El Portillo in the north and Boca de Tauce in the south. To cross at either point is to suddenly enter another world, and to wonder at the force that still simmers beneath the cone of Teide today. Portillo visitor centre is a good place to begin, with a tour of its interactive exhibits that explain vulcanism and the unique environments it creates.

Clockwise from far left: Teide rising above the clouds, seen from Mirador de las Cumbres; Las Cañadas rock formation; the Teleférico; model of a beetle at the visitor centre; alpine flowers dot the rocky slopes of Caldera de las Cañadas; the national park is home to a host of interesting plants

Riding high Although a ride up Teide on the Teleférico cable car provides an impressive view of the crater, visitors should still cross it for a close-up look as the road passes through lava fields, inhospitable and impenetrable jumbles of ragged lava, 'sand' dunes of greenish and red lava pebbles called *picon* and outcrops of red, blue, yellow and black volcanic stone. Frequent lookout points have excellent signage in English.

Walkers take note Teide is surrounded by the Parque Nacional del Teide, which has several hiking trails. One of the most interesting is around the jagged Roques de García, a path that encounters several different types of lava (including the twisted ropes of pahoehoe) and descends a lava flow into the Llano de Uncano plain to the foot of Catedral, a 100m (330ft) rock dome.

THE BASICS

➕ E5

El Portillo visitor centre

🕐 Daily 9–4

🍴 Restaurant El Portilla (€€), Parador cafeteria (€€)

🚌 TITSA buses 342, 348

❓ Daily guided excursions (book in advance, tel 922 29 01 29)

Teleférico

www.teleferico-teide.com

☎ 922 01 04 40

🕐 Daily 9–4, last descent 5

💷 Expensive

More to See

CAMELLO CENTER
www.camellocenter.com

This is a chance to meet and ride camels, once extensively used in local agriculture.

🔢 D4 ✉ Carretera TF82 km10.2, El Tanque ☎ 922 13 61 91 ⏱ Daily 10–5 🍴 Canarian specialties (€–€€) 🚌 TITSA bus 460 ⚑ None 💰 Moderate–expensive

CENTRO ALFARERO DE ARGUAYO AND MUSEO ETNOGRÁFICO

The Centro keeps alive the pottery making traditions of the Guanches, using original designs and firing techniques. The museum displays the island's ethnographic heritage.

🔢 C5 ✉ Carreterra General 35 (TF375), Santiago del Teide ☎ 922 86 34 65 ⏱ Tue–Sun 10–1, 4–7 🚌 TITSA bus 462 ⚑ Few 💰 Free

OASIS DEL VALLE
www.oasisdelvalle.com

Tasteful theme park with banana plantation, gofio mill, museum of Canarian customs, gardens and animals. This eclectic collection includes ostrich, kangaroo, llama, zebra, reptiles and camels to ride.

🔢 G3 ✉ Trasera Camino Torreón 2, El Ramal, La Orotava (exit 33 from TF5) ☎ 922 33 35 09 ⏱ Daily 10–5 🍴 Canarian specialties (€–€€) ⚑ Few 💰 Expensive

LA OROTAVA: JARDINES MARQUESADO DE LA QUINTA ROJA

These colourful 19th-century gardens cover more than 11,600sq m (3 acres) of ravines and terraces, crowned by the mausoleum of Don Diego Castillo, denied church burial because he was a Mason.

🔢 G4 ✉ Calle San Agustin, La Orotava ⏱ May–Oct daily 8am–10pm, Nov–Apr daily 8am–9pm 🍴 Nearby 🚌 TITSA buses 101, 107, 108, 345, 347, 348 ⚑ Few 💰 Moderate

LA OROTAVA: MUSEO DE CERÁMICA

Nearly 1,000 examples of the oldest and most typical Spanish pottery shown in a distinguished

Impressive displays at the Museo de la Cerámica

mansion, with a gallery shop where contemporary pieces are sold.

✚ G4 ✉ Calle Leon 3, La Orotava ☎ 922 32 14 47 🕔 Mon–Sat 10–6, Sun 10–2 🍴 Plaza de la Constitución 🚌 TITSA buses 101, 107, 108, 345, 348 ♿ None ✋ Inexpensive

LA OROTAVA: NUESTRA SEÑORA DE LA CONCEPCIÓN

Built between 1768 and 1788 to replace the original 1503 church, this is the most pure baroque church on the island. Twin towers flank a unique façade. It has a textile collection as well as collections of gold, silver and jewels.

✚ G4 ✉ Plaza de Casañas 🕔 Variable 🚌 TITSA buses 101, 107, 108, 345, 347, 348 ♿ Few ✋ Free

PUEBLO CHICO

www.pueblochico.com

Tenerife in miniature, where you feel like a giant towering over mountains and buildings. Sections depict the island beginnings, Guanche culture, colonial times and major places and buildings.

✚ F4 ✉ Autopiste del Norte (TF5) exit 35, La Orotava ☎ 922 33 40 60 🕔 Daily 9–7 (till 6pm in winter) 🍴 On site (€) ♿ Good ✋ Expensive

PUERTO DE LA CRUZ: IGLESIA SAN FRANCISCO/SAN JUAN BAUTISTA

The oldest remaining building in the city (1599) is this former church, whose main altar of red, green and gold is now the backdrop for concerts. Above the altar is a Mudejar ceiling in the sanctuary.

✚ F3 ✉ Calle Quintana, Puerto de la Cruz 🕔 Daily 🍴 Nearby Plaza del Charco ♿ Good ✋ Free

PUERTO DE LA CRUZ: JARDÍN TAORO

The steeply terraced Taoro Gardens could use some upkeep, but are still worth wandering in on your way to or from Jardín Acuático Risco Bello (▷ 60–61), just above. A stone bridge crosses a pool between waterfalls and a mirador

Puerto de la Cruz is known for its lava pools

Bright poinsettias at Taoro Park

overlooks the city. There's a small playground below the café. Just above, behind the hotel, is Taoro Park, a large open green space popular with runners.

✚ F3 ✉ Carretera Taoro, Puerto de la Cruz 🕐 Daylight hours 🍴 Restaurant-café in gardens (€) ♿ None 🎫 Free

PUERTO DE LA CRUZ: MUSEO ARQUEOLÓGICO

Arresting displays illustrate the life and arts of Tenerife's aboriginal people. Visitors feel as though they were actually looking into a Guanche burial cave. Good English sign translations are provided.

✚ F3 ✉ Calle Lomo 28, Puerto de la Cruz ☎ 922 37 14 65 🕐 Tue–Sat 10–1, 5–9, Sun 10–1 🍴 Several nearby ♿ Good 🎫 Inexpensive

PUERTO DE LA CRUZ: NUESTRA SEÑORA DE LA PEÑA DE FRANCIA

Two gold-covered carved wood altars and a large chased silver cross on the left side wall are among the treasures of the 1684 church. Outside is a leafy plaza with benches overlooking the church, flower beds and a large fountain surmounted by a swan.

✚ F3 ✉ Plaza de la Iglesia, Puerto de la Cruz ☎ 922 38 00 51 🕐 Mon–Sat 3–7, Sun 9–7 🍴 Several nearby ♿ Few 🎫 Free

PUERTO DE LA CRUZ: PLAYA JARDÍN

Puerto de la Cruz's main beach, a 1km (0.5-mile) strand of dark volcanic sand distinguished by palms and extensive cactus gardens, is the work of architect César Manrique. It begins at the end of the commercial harbour and extends as far west as Loro Parque. Showers and changing cabanas are at the beach, which is protected by an artificial reef from pounding by the serious surf that characterizes the north shore.

✚ F3 ✉ Avenida Carillo 🕐 Daily 🍴 Cafés 🚌 TITSA bus 381 ♿ Good 🎫 Free

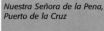

Nuestra Señora de la Pena, Puerto de la Cruz

Dark sand beach of Playa Jardín

Puerto de la Cruz

Puerto de la Cruz's old town clusters along its craggy waterfront. Outdoor cafés, shady plazas and fine old buildings line its streets.

DISTANCE: 1km (0.6 miles) **ALLOW:** 1.5 hours, with stops

START

TOURIST INFORMATION OFFICE
➕ F3

1 Begin by picking up a map of the town at the tourist office in Casa de la Aduana, the restored former customs house, built in 1620.

2 Walk around the little enclosed harbour of Puerto Pesquero, past sculptor Julio Nieto's statue of a fisherwoman, unveiled in 2008. Little fishing boats are usually pulled up on the shore below.

3 Follow the harbour around to the right, then follow the wide Calle la Marina to the left, into Plaza del Charco. This tree-lined square is the heart of Puerto de la Cruz, lively at any time of day or night.

4 Leave the square at the opposite side, on Calle Blanco, and follow it to Calle Iriarte. Go left into Plaza Concejil, surrounded by three examples of traditional Canarian architecture.

END

PLAZA REYES CATOLICAS
➕ F3

8 Leave the church by the side door, turning right to emerge at the terrace overlooking the sea. Follow Paseo de San Telmo along the rocky seafront to the tiny white Ermita San Telmo, a church built by sailors, at Plaza Reyes Catolicos.

7 Join locals for a rest in this shady spot before visiting the adjacent church of Nuestra Señora de la Peña de Francia (▷ 70).

6 Follow Calle Cologan into the charming little Plaza de la Iglesia, where benches face a stone fountain topped by a swan.

5 Follow the flower-decked Calle Iriarte (named for a major Spanish writer, whose birthplace on the plaza is now a souvenir shop), to Calle Cologan and turn left.

THE WEST

WALK

Shopping

AQUA Y SOL
Expensive little bikinis and beachwear for women and men.
➕ F3 ✉ Calle de la Hoya 38, Puerto de la Cruz 🕒 Mon–Fri 10–1, 4.30–7.30, Sat 10–1

ARTENERIFE KIOSKO PUERTO DE LA CRUZ
The striking contemporary kiosk at the old harbour shows off a fine selection of crafts.
➕ F3 ✉ Explanada del Muelle, Puerto de la Cruz ☎ 922 38 82 02

LA CASA DEL DRAGO
A rambling shop adjoining the Drago tree park, filled with all the Tenerife specialties: lace, pottery and food items.
➕ D4 ✉ Arcipreste 3, Icod de los Vinos ☎ 922 81 04 51 🚍 TITSA buses 107, 108, 325

CASA LERCARO EN LA OROTAVA
Traditional homeware gifts and jewellery in a 17th-century mansion. There is also a restaurant and wine shop.
➕ G4 ✉ Calle Colegio 5–7, Orotava ☎ 922 32 62 04 🕒 Closed Sun 🚍 TITSA buses 101, 107, 108, 345, 347

CASA DE REGALO
Excellent selection of hand-made items from Latin America, including children's clothes, embroidery, Panama hats and jewellery.
➕ F3 ✉ Calle de la Hoya 60, Puerto de la Cruz 🚍 TITSA

bus 381 between Lago Martiánez and Playa Jardín

CENTRO ALFARERO DE ARGUAYO
Buy Guanche-style pottery made without a wheel directly from the potters.
➕ C3 ✉ Carretera General 35 (TF375), Santiago del Teide (near Los Gigantes) ☎ 922 86 34 65 🕒 Tue–Sun 10–1, 4–7 🚍 TITSA bus 462

ESSENZA ARTE Y ARTESANIAS
Two galleries show some of the island's best and most unusual crafts, with smart contemporary designs in ceramics, fiber, wood, metals and leather.
➕ F3 ✉ Calle Quintana 3, Puerto de la Cruz ☎ 922 38 56 77 ✉ Plaza de Charco 6, Puerto de la Cruz ☎ 922 38 88 21

FUND GRUBE
Watches, fashion accessories and perfumes in

STREET MARKETS
Lively and filled with bargains for careful shoppers, markets are entertaining and a good source of everyday needs. Puerto de la Cruz has two (🕒 Mon, Sat 8–4), and Buenavista del Norte, on the northwest coast, has a popular one (🕒 Sun 9.30–1.30). Farmers' markets are a good source of self-catering provisions and local food specialties; La Orotava has a good one on Saturdays (🕒 9–2).

the Shopping Center Martiánez.
➕ F3 ✉ Avenida de Colón 12, Puerto de la Cruz 🕒 Daily 9.30am–10pm

MODAS DIOLAE
Factory showrooms sell leather gloves, belts, handbags, shoes, briefcases, wallets and boots.
➕ F3 ✉ Carretera Vieja 12, Puerto de la Cruz ☎ 922 30 18 18 🚍 Free bus half-hourly 9–6 from Avenida Venezuela

NATIONAL PARK VISITORS CENTRE
The tiny shop is crammed with excellent books (in English) on all the islands, nature guides, tasteful T-shirts and clothing, hiking maps, lava jewellery and snacks.
➕ F5 ✉ El Portillo, TF21 🚍 TITSA buses 342, 348

PIRAMIDES MARTIÁNEZ MALL
Mall with two levels of shops selling clothing, electronics, sporting goods, beachwear, perfumes and more.
➕ F3 ✉ Avenida Generalisimo, Puerto de la Cruz 🕒 Mon–Sat 10–9, Sun 10–8 🚍 TITSA bus 381

PRODUCTOS DE LA TIERRA
Traditional Canarian food specialties including unusual liquors, *mojo* sauces, wines and the unique Canarian *gofio*.
➕ F3 ✉ Calle Santo Domingo 7, Puerto de la Cruz ☎ 922 38 55 71

Entertainment and Activities

ABAMA GOLF

www.abamahotelresort.com

Designed by Dave Thomas with views of the sea below, this 18-hole par 72 course opened in 2005. The resort complex is vast and a tasteful shade of fluorescent pink.

🞤 C6 ⊠ TF 47 (km 9), Guia de Isora ☎ 922 12 63 00 🕓 Daily tee-off 8–2 🚌 TITSA bus 462, 493

EL ARADO

This restaurant-bar with tables outside is a good place to go for live Canarian and South American music.

🞤 F3 ⊠ Calle Puerto Viejo 22, Puerto de la Cruz ☎ 922 37 30 85 🕓 Live music 8.30–midnight

BUENAVISTA GOLF

www.buenavistagolf.es

In the extreme northwest corner of the island, the 18-hole par 72 course has spectacular views along the coast.

🞤 C4 ⊠ Calle La Finca, Buenavista del Norte ☎ 922 12 90 34 🚌 TITSA bus 107, 355, 363

CABALLO BLANCO

This club continues to be popular, especially with a slightly older crowd and comes as a bit of a relief from the usual thumping nightspot. There's a keyboard player as well as a DJ. The music harps back to the 1960s to 80s.

🞤 F3 ⊠ San Telmo, Puerto del la Cruz ☎ 922 38 56 56 🕓 Tue–Sun 9pm–3am

EL CARDÓN TURISMO ACTIVO

www.elcardon.com

Outdoor sports include kayaking, mountain biking, snorkelling, hiking, climbing and caving in volcanic tubes plus guided trips to Punta del Teno, Los Gigantes and Garachico.

🞤 C4 ⊠ Plaza de los Remedios 2, Buenavista del Norte ☎ 922 12 79 38, 902 45 55 50 (reservations) 🕓 Daily by reservation 🚌 TITSA bus 107, 363

COURTYARD CABARET BAR

English is spoken at this friendly bar which also offers live music.

🞤 C6 ⊠ Centro Comercial Santiago, Puerto de Santiago ☎ 922 86 24 03 🕓 Daily 7pm–early morning

DIVE SHOPS

PADI-certified instructors guide experienced divers or train new ones. Ocean Blue Divers' Gold Palm instructors work daily with age 10 and up, from Puerto Santiago (⊠ Calle Caleta del Jurado, Jardines del Mar ☎ 922 86 24 02; www.oceanbluedivers.com 🕓 Daily 9.30–6 🚌 TITSA bus 473, 477). In Puerto de la Cruz, El Cardumen operates multiple diving expeditions daily (⊠ Avenida Melchor Luz 3 ☎ 922 36 84 68, 670 38 30 07; www.elcardumen. com). Both have sales and rental shops.

MIXTURE

A raucous disco pub, where the fun starts late and ends early—in the morning.

🞤 F3 ⊠ Calle Iriarte 58, Puerto de la Cruz 🕓 Wed–Sat from 10pm

PLAZA DEL CHARCO

Puerto de la Cruz's nightlife centres around this large square filled with cafés, music and activity. Everyone gravitates here, to sit in its cafés, listen to music, buy from street vendors, eat in the restaurants or just stroll its perimeter after dinner.

🞤 F3 ⊠ Puerto de la Cruz 🚌 Central bus station nearby

TENERIFE PALACE

www.tenerifepalace.com

Performances might be flamenco, ballet, bands or acrobats. The intimate hall seats just 550.

🞤 F3 ⊠ Camino del Coche, Puerto de la Cruz ☎ 922 37 40 11, 922 38 29 60

TENOACTIVO

www.tenoactivo.com

Sea kayaking instruction for all levels, kayak tours and equipment rental for independent exploration (for groups of experienced kayakers only) of the coast. Teno also lead guided hiking trips into the mountains and offer dive shop services.

🞤 C4 ⊠ La Alhóndiga 45, Buenavista del Norte ☎ 922 12 80 60 🚌 TITSA buses 108, 335, 363

Restaurants

PRICES

Prices are approximate, based on a 3-course meal for one person.

€€€	over €25
€€	€15–€25
€	under €15

BODEGON DE LOS COMPADRES €€

Traditional Canarian food in a casual atmosphere.

✚ G4 ✉ Calle Claudio 9, La Orotava ☎ 922 33 51 53 ◷ Tue–Sun 12–12 ▢ TITSA buses 101, 107, 108, 345, 348

BODEGON MATIAS €€

Locally famed for its chorizo, baked cheese with four sauces and rabbit *salmorejo*.

✚ G4 ✉ Calle Guanche 2, Los Pinos, La Orotava (Carretera General near La Florida turn) ☎ 922 32 02 59 ◷ Lunch, dinner ▢ TITSA bus 345

CAFÉ ARENA €–€€

Londoners serve English breakfast, Sunday roast, scones and sandwiches—without TV.

✚ C6 ✉ Avenida Marítima, Playa de la Arena ☎ 687 87 73 67 ◷ Thu–Tue from 8.30am ▢ TITSA buses 473, 477

CASA JUANA €–€€

Long established and popular for seafood.

✚ C6 ✉ Calle Virgen de Candelaria 13, Alcalá ☎ 922 86 61 26 ◷ Lunch, dinner ▢ TITSA buses 473, 477

ESCONDIDA €€

www.escondida.es
Eclectic fusion cuisine in a stylish setting with harbour views.

✚ C6 ✉ Calle Pasaje el Ancla 1, Alcalá ☎ 922 86 50 80 ◷ Wed–Mon lunch, dinner ▢ TITSA buses 473, 477

MIL SABORES €€

Creative Mediterranean cuisine is served here, making good use of fresh local products. Baked vine-ripened Canarian tomatoes are stuffed with vegetables and goat's cheese, and *pongo,* a white fish, is served with a tangy mango sauce. Excellent Canarian house wine and a helpful and amiable waitstaff help make this an outstanding break from traditional fare.

✚ F3 ✉ Calle Cruz Verde 5, Puerto de la Cruz ☎ 922 36 81 72 ◷ Thu–Tue 6.30–11, Sat–Sun 12.30–3, 6.30–11

ORGANIC AND VEGETARIAN

Natural and organic foods, while certainly not unknown on the island, are not widely embraced by restaurants. Puerto de la Cruz has one shining exception. El Mana provides a haven for vegetarians and those who revel in dishes made with natural and organically grown ingredients. ✉ Calle Mequínez 21 ☎ 922 37 24 74; www.elmanacocinanatural.com ◷ 1–4, 7–11

RESTAURANTE REGULO €€

www.restauranteregulo.com
Canarian ingredients fuse with mainland Spanish style in a starter of piquillo peppers stuffed with grouper, or octopus carpaccio.

✚ F3 ✉ Pérez Zamora 16, Puerto de la Cruz ☎ 922 38 45 06 ◷ Mon 6–11pm, Tue–Sat 12–3, 6–11

RESTAURANTE RUSTICO €–€€

Tucked under an arcade at the start of the Paseo, overlooking the coastal surf, Rustico serves shrimp, calamari and other seafood.

✚ F3 ✉ Paseo San Telmo 1, Puerto de la Cruz ☎ 922 37 37 92 ◷ Daily 12–12

LA ROSA DI BARI €€–€€€

www.larosadibari.com
A lovely location for a romantic dinner. Innovative food using the finest ingredients.

✚ F3 ✉ Calle Lomo 23, Puerto del la Cruz ☎ 922 36 85 23 ◷ Tue–Sat lunch, dinner, Sun lunch

VICTORIA RESTAURANTE & TASCA €€

Canarian dishes are served here in a 16th-century home that's also a small *hotel rurale* (▷ 111).

✚ G4 ✉ Hermano Apolinar 8, La Orotava ◷ Dinner only ☎ 922 33 16 83 ▢ TITSA buses 101, 107, 108 345, 347, 348

Beaches and spring-like temperatures in midwinter are the hallmarks of Tenerife's southern coast, which not long ago was a barren landscape broken by scattered fishing villages and banana plantations. Today lively resorts attract visitors to its beaches.

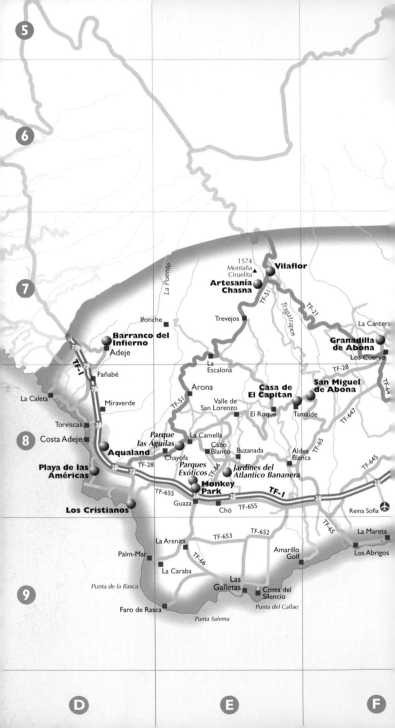

Los Cristianos and Playa de las Américas

HIGHLIGHTS

- Playa del Duque
- Las Américas nightlife
- Boat trips from Los Cristianos
- Playa de las Vistas
- Strolling the streets of Los Cristianos

TIPS

- Bus stops are rarely close to beaches–get a bus map.
- For the best scenery, walk the seafront promenade from Playa Fañabé around to Playa del Duque.

These busy beach enclaves filled with people enjoying the south coast's ample sun and imported sand are most people's idea of what Tenerife is like. They are not disappointed when they arrive.

Close, but different Los Cristianos and Las Américas blend together, and in turn blend into Costa Adeje to the west, where development around Playa del Duque covers the hillsides in luxury resorts. Shops at Plaza Playa del Duque, restaurants and even the beach and garden-lined promenade reflect the upscale tastes (and budgets) of those who congregate here. At Las Américas is the sport harbour of Puerto Colón and a concentration of hotels, restaurants and nightlife that draws both a hip young crowd and package-holiday guests to its lively bars, pubs and clubs.

Clockwise from far left: Café terrace in Playa de las Américas; fort complex, Las Américas; hotels and apartment blocks line this stretch of coast; sign for Las Américas' aquarium; pedestrian street, Los Cristianos; view out to sea from Las Américas

Beautiful beaches A string of beaches line the coast, with public access clearly marked. Only Los Cristianos, at the eastern end, existed before tourism arrived. It still has the feel of that real town with narrow streets winding up from the harbour, where fishermen sell their daily catch. Kiosks sell fishing, sailing, diving or whale- and dolphin-watch cruises. Its relaxed family-oriented clientele enjoys the golden sands of Playa de Las Vistas (brought in from the Sahara), adjoining the harbour for inter-island ferries.

In the hills Above the coast, small towns and villages cling to the steep hillsides that rise to Mount Teide. The largest—Vilaflor, San Miguel, Adeje and Granadilla—make excellent low-key bases for exploring the region and Mount Teide, especially for hikers.

THE BASICS

www.costa-adeje.es

✚ D8

🍴 Plentiful

🚌 TITSA buses 111 from airport; 110 or 111 from Santa Cruz

♿ Playa de las Vistas beach access excellent; Playa Fañabé and Playa del Duque also good

ℹ Centro Cultural del Pescador 1, Los Cristianos, tel 922 75 71 37; Mon–Fri 9–3.30, Sat 9–1

Vilaflor

HIGHLIGHTS

● Iglesia de San Pedro
● Ermita de San Roque lookout
● Pino Gordo (giant pine)
● Local wines

TIPS

● Vilaflor's altitude makes it a good base for summer travels, when the coast is much hotter.
● The tasting bar at Artesanía Chasna (▷ 82) allows visitors to compare local wines.

Vilaflor lives up to its name, with flowers everywhere: in dooryards, along the top of walls and in little plots along Calle Santa Catalina. Along with flowers, Vilaflor grows potatoes and wine grapes—in Europe's highest vineyards.

Sainted son The town, like the land above and below, is largely vertical, so that even its main square, Plaza de San Pedro, lies at a slant. At one side is the mansion of the town's founder, Captain Pedro Soler, with an enclosed wooden balcony along its entire façade. Opposite stands the grey stone church he financed, dedicated to the town's favourite son, Brother Pedro de San José de Betancourt, founder of the Order of the Hospitallers of Bethlehem, born here in 1626 and canonized in 2002. Inside, the church has

View of Vilaflor from above (top left); Californian poppies (bottom left); the steep terrain means crops have to be grown in terraces (right)

its original carved wood ceiling and balcony, as well as the original 17th-century font in which San Pedro was baptized.

Pine and wine Above the town the Corona Forestal spills down from the slopes of Teide. This vast forest of Canarian pine (*Pinus canariensis*) ends with one of the largest known of this species, in a little park overlooking the *barranco* as the road climbs out of town. Only the top two-thirds of its 70m (230ft) height can be seen from the road; stop at the *mirador* to appreciate Pino Gordo and walk down to the little park around its enormous trunk. Along with strolling Vilaflor's flower-painted streets and enjoying its cool mountain air, visitors can sample the products of Spain's highest town at the bodegas of Lajial and Zeveron.

THE BASICS

✚ E7
✉ TF21 or TF51
🍽 Several
🚌 TITSA bus 482
♿ Few

More to See

AQUALAND
www.aqualand.es
The supercharged waterpark has a dolphin lake and show with 15 bottle-nosed dolphins, and water rides and slides that twist, spin and splash all ages. There are separate rides for younger children. The park is very popular with families.

✚ D8 ✉ Avenida Austria 15, Costa Adeje; exit 29 from TF1 ☎ 922 71 52 66 🕐 Daily 10–5 🍴 Several (€–€€) 🚌 Free bus from Los Cristianos and Playa de las Américas ♿ Few 💷 Very expensive ❓ Dolphin shows daily at 3pm

ARICO EL NUEVO
A narrow street drops from the C822 to tidy little Plaza de la Luz, a quadrangle of freshly whitewashed buildings facing a small 18th-century church. The whole timeless village is a protected historic site. At Arico Villa, the otherwise traditional Canarian church has a baroque façade, an unusual onion dome and elaborate altar (the town hall, opposite, has the key).

✚ G7 🍴 Tasquita Pimenton (€€, ▷ 90) 🚌 TITSA bus 430 ♿ None ℹ Calle Beniez de Lugo 1, Arico Villa, tel 922 16 11 33; Mon–Fri 9–2.30

ARTESANÍA CHASNA
This hillside complex celebrates all the island's arts with a free audiovisual show, Canarian music, a tasting bar where you can sample Vilaflor wines and one of the island's best selections of local crafts and food products.

✚ E7 ✉ TF51 at Vilaflor ☎ 922 70 91 75 🕐 Sun–Fri 9–6 🍴 Tasting bar with light foods 🚌 TITSA bus 482 ♿ Good

BARRANCO DEL INFIERNO
www.barrancodelinfierno.es
Only 200 walkers are admitted each day to this deep ravine with flora and fauna unique in world. The *barranco* has Tenerife's only year-round river, a waterfall and the island's highest willow forest.

✚ D7 ✉ Calle El Molino, Adeje ☎ 922 78 28 85 🕐 Entry to path 8.30–2.30 daily, open until 5.30; reserve in advance 🍴 Otelo

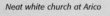
Neat white church at Arico

The entrance to the Barranco del Infierno

(€€, ▷ 90) 🚌 TITSA bus 473 from Los Cristianos 🚫 None 👐 Inexpensive

GRANADILLA DE ABONA

www.granadilladeabona.org/turismo
Brightly painted buildings make a striking view, clinging to the steep hillside. Granadilla provides exceptional tourist information, including a free guide (in English) to walking trails exploring abandoned villages, Guanche caves of Chiñama and the geological site of Paisaje Lunar (moonscape). The town hall is in a 17th-century convent (Mon–Sat 10–2, Mon–Fri 5–7).

➕ F7 ✉ TF21, TF28, TF64 🍴 El Terrero, (€€, ▷ 90) 🚌 TITSA bus 130 from Santa Cruz, 470 from Los Cristianos 🚫 None ℹ Plaza de El Médano, El Médano, tel 922 17 60 02; Mon–Fri 9–3, Sat 9–1; shorter summer hours

JARDINES DEL ATLANTICO BANANERA

Visitors see a banana plantation on guided tours of this family farm, learning about crops, animals and local culture, and sampling banana liquor and honey rum.

➕ E8 ✉ TF1 exit 26, Buzanada ☎ 922 72 04 03 🕐 Mon–Fri 10–6 🍴 None 🚌 Free bus from Los Cristianos and Playa de las Américas 🚫 Few 👐 Moderate

MONKEY PARK

www.monkeypark.com
More varieties of monkey and their cousins than you probably knew existed, in a pleasant setting where visitors can walk among some of them and feed them, often out of your hand. Take some fruit to share or buy the standard feed there (the animals seem to welcome some variety!).

➕ E8 ✉ Llano Azul 17, off TF1 between Guia and Los Cristianos ☎ 922 79 07 20 🕐 Daily 9.30–5 🍴 Very limited; bring your own snacks 🚌 TITSA buses 112, 467, 470, 473 🚫 Few 👐 Expensive

PARQUE LAS ÁGUILAS

www.aguilasjunglepark.com
A tropical jungle filled with mammals, reptiles and birds. The raptor

Indian langur monkey with newborn baby at Monkey Park

Statue at Parque Las Águilas

show features free-flying hawks, buzzards and a bald eagle. Penguins, hippopotami, lions, tigers and various primates live in natural settings, some with rope bridges to try.

➕ E8 ✉ Urbanización Las Águilas del Teide ☎ 922 72 90 10 🕐 Daily 10–5.30, last ticket 4.30 🍴 Several 🚌 Free bus from Los Cristianos and Playa de las Américas ♿ Few ✋ Very expensive ❓ Exotic bird shows at 11, 2, 5; birds of prey shows at noon and 4

PARQUES EXÓTICOS (AMAZONIA)

Exotic tropical gardens plus a domed building house an Amazonian jungle-like environment with birds and reptiles.

➕ E8 ✉ TF1 exit 26 ☎ 922 79 54 24 🕐 Daily 10–6 🚌 Free hourly bus from Playa de las Américas and Los Cristianos ♿ Few ✋ Expensive

SAN MIGUEL DE ABONA

www.sanmigueldeabona.org

In hills above the coast, San Miguel seems far away from the busy

resorts, and is a good base for travellers not keen on the pubs-and-clubs scene. Two par-72 golf courses attract golfers. Near Mirador La Centinela, where there are enticing views of the whole coast, a trail leads to prehistoric engravings.

➕ F8 ✉ TF28 🍴 several (€–€€) 🚌 TITSA buses 116, 416, 484 ♿ Few ℹ Avenida Galván Bello, Golf del Sur, tel 922 73 86 64; Mon–Fri 9–11.30, 12–5.30, Sat 9.30–1.30

SAN MIGUEL DE ABONA: CASA DE EL CAPITAN

www.sanmigueldeabona.org

The Captain's House is a modern museum of local life and culture in a restored 18th-century home, filled with traditional and contemporary pottery, wine, camels, farming, and local crafts and art.

➕ E8 ✉ Calle El Calvario 1, San Miguel de Abona ☎ 922 16 72 58 or 922 70 08 87 🕐 Mon–Fri 9–2.30, 5–7.30, Sat 10–2 🍴 Nearby 🚌 TITSA buses 116, 416, 484 ♿ None ✋ Inexpensive

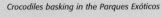

Crocodiles basking in the Parques Exóticos

San Miguel de Abona is known for golf

A Walk in Adeje

The hill town of Adeje is the centre of local life and its outdoor cafés are popular with walkers visiting the Barranco del Infierno.

DISTANCE: 1km (0.6 miles) **ALLOW:** 1.5 hours, with stops

START

CALLE GRANDE
 D7 TITSA bus 473

① Begin at the foot of Calle Grande, Adeje's lively main street, and walk uphill, through the many casual cafés that sprawl across the pavement.

② Step inside Hotel Fonda Central (▷ 110), on the left, to see typical Canarian buildings with balconied patios.

③ Continue along Calle Grande, crossing to enter Plaza de España, beside the church. The Franciscan convent on the right, founded in 1679, has been restored as the Ayuntamiento (town hall), and only its church remains.

④ Cross the plaza to enter the church of St Ursula, built in the 16th and 17th centuries, with Mudejar coffered ceilings, painted and gold altars and a baptistery set inside a carved wood grille.

END

BARRANCO DEL INFIERNO
 D7 TITSA bus 473

⑦ Continue uphill to the entrance to Barranco del Infierno (▷ 82), whose almost vertical walls enclose a river, waterfall, willow forest and plants unique to this spot. Good signage explains many details of the *barranco*, and the terrace provides good views if you have not reserved a hiking time for the trail.

⑥ From Casa Fuerte, continue up the steep hill to the right, catching your breath and admiring the vertiginous views at the terrace of Otelo (▷ 90).

⑤ On leaving the church, turn left at the end of the street, walking to Casa Fuerte, the 16th-century bastion of the counts of Gomera and built to protect the family and African slaves from pirate attacks. A path leads around the lower walls.

THE SOUTH

WALK

The Southern Mountains

This drive climbs the shoulder of Mount Teide to Spain's highest town, Vilaflor, with sweeping views to the coast below.

DISTANCE: 42km (26 miles) **ALLOW:** 3 hours, with stops

START

SAN MIGUEL DE ABONA
✛ F8

❶ Leave from Casa de El Capitan (▷ 84), driving downhill to the main street, the TF28, and turn left.

❷ Follow the TF28 through the small business centre of San Miguel, climbing out of town and crossing several deep ravines before reaching the terraced town of Charco de Pino.

❸ Continue on to Granadilla (right), stopping in Plaza Iglesia to walk up well-kept Calle Iglesia with its brightly painted homes.

❹ From Granadilla follow the TF21 north (signposted Teide Vilaflor); the road is lined with eucalyptus trees as it climbs through increasingly steep pastures with far-reaching views. Pass the wine town of Cruz de Tea, at 850m (2,788ft) elevation.

END

SAN MIGUEL DE ABONA

❽ Turn right onto the TF565, enjoying views of the coast and of El Roque, on the right shortly before the TF565 ends at the TF28. A left turn brings you back to San Miguel.

❼ Turn right onto the TF51 (signposted Arona), stopping to see local crafts at Artesanía Chasna (▷ 82) and continue through the terraced vineyards to La Espalona.

❻ Continue through Vilaflor, staying right at the intersection of the TF51, to the *mirador* above the town. After stopping for views, return to Vilaflor.

❺ Above, the road becomes even steeper before entering a pine forest. After the Donna Marta lookout, negotiate the series of 180-degree turns, where you can see layers of road directly below and above.

Shopping

ARTENERIFE KIOSKO PLAYA DE LAS AMÉRICAS

Pottery, including Guanche replicas, and various fibre arts, all island-made.

➕ D8 ✉ Avenida de Rafael Puig Liuvina, Playa de las Américas ☎ 922 79 43 43
🚌 TITSA buses 416, 417, 487

ARTENERIFE KIOSKO PUERTO COLÓN

A good selection of high-quality authentic island crafts, including woodcarving and fretwork.

➕ D8 ✉ Avenida Gran Britania, Zona de Ochio, Adeje ☎ 922 79 75 06 🚌 TITSA bus 473

ARTENERIFE KIOSKO LAS VISTAS

Island art and crafts, most using local materials, including lava, pine wood and banana leaves.

➕ D8 ✉ Playa de las Vistas, Los Cristianos ☎ 922 75 00 98

ARTESANÍA CHASNA

One of the island's best selections of local crafts, including carvings from black lava stone, banana-leaf collages, pottery, and local food (▷ 82).

➕ E7 ✉ TF51 Vilaflor ☎ 922 70 91 75 🕐 Sun–Fri 9–6 🚌 TITSA bus 482 ♿ Good

BLAZERS BOUTIQUE

Women's clothing in all the latest continental styles at very reasonable prices.

➕ D8 ✉ Calle Juan XXIII 10, Los Cristianos ☎ 922 79 31 94 🕐 Mon–Sat 10–8, Sun 2–8

BOOKSWOP

You can exchange your English books here or buy secondhand.

➕ D8 ✉ Commerical Centre Puerto Colon, Playa Las Americas ☎ 922 71 56 82 🕐 Mon–Sat 10–6 🚌 TITSA 342, 343, 416, 417, 467, 487

COSTA ADEJE MARKET

Expect to find just about everything in this big twice-weekly marketplace near the El Duque shopping centre. It combines farmers' market, local craftsmen, general market stalls and vendors selling goods from Africa, including Moroccan leather.

➕ D8 ✉ Avenida de Bruelas at Plaza Jardines del Duque 🕐 Thu, Sat 9–2 🚌 TITSA buses 111, 342, 343

SHOP HOURS

Shop hours vary, and may change often, with many smaller boutiques closing for a midday break but staying open into the evening. In resort towns (except in shopping complexes) typical shop hours are Mon–Fri 10–1.30 and 5.30–9, Sat 10–2, often closed Sun. Others are open Mon–Sat 10–9 without break, although Saturday afternoon closings are common. Hours are longer and usually continuous in shopping malls.

PUNTA ROMA

Stylish women's clothing, with an eye to fashionable colour coordinates.

➕ D8 ✉ Avenida de Suecia 17, Los Cristianos 🕐 Mon–Sat 10–9

ROSAS

Beautifully embroidered and appliquéd clothing and household linens which are better quality than found at most beach-front bazaars.

➕ D8 ✉ Calle Pabos Abril 1, Los Cristianos

SAN EUGENIO SHOPPING CENTRE

A complex with a selection of duty free shops and fashion stores such as Mango. There is a large underground supermarket and car park.

➕ D8 ✉ San Eugenio, Playa de las Americas 🚌 TITSA 342, 343, 416, 417, 467, 487

SIKKIM

This little shop offers unusual clothes, jewellery and accessories for women, with a resident tailor on hand to make sure they fit just right.

➕ D8 ✉ Avenida de Suecia 9, Los Cristianos 🕐 Mon–Sat 10–2, 4.30–8.30

VERDE

This tiny shop has table linens and clothing embroidered in bright traditional designs.

➕ D8 ✉ Calle Barranquillo 27, Los Cristianos 🕐 Mon–Sat 10–1.30, 4.30–8.30

Entertainment and Activities

AMARILLA GOLF AND COUNTRY CLUB

www.amarillagolf.es
This challenging Donald Steel-designed par-72, 18-hole course with sea views has full services; it only rains three days a year here.

⊞ E9 ✉ TF1 exit 24, towards the sea; take first right ☎ 922 73 03 19 🕔 Daily 🚍 TITSA buses 116, 484

BARAKUDA CLUB TENERIFE

www.diving-tenerife.com
For more than 20 years the Club has provided diving equipment rentals, and trips.

⊞ D8 ✉ Hotel Paraiso Floral, Largo Playa Paraiso, Costa Adeje ☎ 922 74 18 81 🚍 TITSA buses 472, 473

BIKE POINT EL MÉDANO

www.medanobike.com
Road and mountain bikes and GPS units, rental, sales and service. Guided and unguided tours available. There are six styles of bike available.

⊞ G8 ✉ Calle Villa Orotava 10, El Médano ☎ 922 17 62 73 🚍 TITSA buses 116, 470, 483

GOLF DEL SUR

www.golfdelsur.es
The golf course underwent a major renovation in 2005. Covering more than 80,000sq m (860,000sq ft), it offers challenging water obstacles and black volcanic sand traps.

⊞ F8 ✉ Galván Bello, San Miguel de Abona ☎ 922 73 81 70 🕔 Daily 🚍 TITSA buses 116, 484

LA ISLA MUSIC

www.laislamusic.com
Cutting-edge technical equipment makes this place popular. Expect R&B and electro on week nights and Sundays, hiphop and electro on Fridays and electro house on Saturdays.

⊞ D8 ✉ Avenida Rafael Puig, Commercial Centre Verónicas 2 (lower level) at Playa de Troya, Las Américas ☎ 922 79 14 84 🕔 Tue–Sun 10pm–5am

MAR DE ONS SEA EXCURSIONS

www.mardeons-tenerife.com
Options range from two-hour photo safaris to three- or five-hour sport fishing trips and sailing excursions that include lunch, swimming and dolphin watching.

THE PERFECT WAVE

El Médano, just east of Tenerife Sur Airport, is one of the world's finest surfing locations, with about 260 days a year with force 4 or stonger winds. Two bays provide different conditions and challenges. El Médano is also popular for windsurfing and sailing. It is perfect for the new sport of kiteboarding. If you don't want to participate, it's great just watching.

⊞ D8 ✉ Puerto de Los Cristianos (at ferry port) ☎ 922 75 15 76 🕔 Daily 🚍 Courtesy bus from 28 locations

LA PIRAMIDE

Located in the Cleopatra Palace Hotel, La Piramide accompanies fine dining with chamber music performed by a live quartet (Mon, Wed, Thu) or opera (Tue, Fri, Sat).

⊞ D8 ✉ Avenida de las Américas, Playa de las Américas ☎ 922 75 75 49 🕔 Performances Mon, Wed, Fri 8.30, Tue, Thu, Sat 9.30 (half an hour earlier in winter) 🚍 TITSA buses 342, 416, 417, 450, 467, 472, 477, 483, 487

ST EUGEN'S

Big and lively, this bar/restaurant puts on live entertainment, live football broadcasts, pool and games for kids.

⊞ D8 ✉ San Eugenio, Playa de las Américas (opposite the shopping centre) ☎ 922 71 33 76 🕔 Mon–Fri 5pm–early hours; Sat–Sun noon–early hours 🚍 TITSA buses 342, 343, 416, 417, 467, 487

TRAMPS

www.trampstenerife.com
Tramps calls itself the king of clubs, and it draws top DJs to the main stage and dance floor. The light show is stupendous. Entrance is free unless a name DJ is there.

⊞ D8 ✉ Starco Centre, Las Américas ☎ 922 79 53 37 🕔 Daily midnight–6am

Restaurants

ASADOR PORTILLO €€

Grilled meats are a specialty, served on tableside grills; the good tapas selection includes garlic shrimp.

✚ D7 ✉ Calle El Portillo 19, San Miguel de Abona ☎ 922 16 70 35 🕐 Tue–Sun lunch, dinner 🚌 TITSA bus 342

CHIRINGO ATLANTICO €

Grilled chicken or local fish on the beach near the ferry quay. Sluggish service, but great location.

✚ D8 ✉ Playa de las Vistas, Los Cristianos 🕐 Daily lunch, dinner ♿ Very good

LA CUEVA €–€€

Children are treated to the same fine service as their parents at this friendly Italian restaurant.

✚ F9 ✉ San Blas Centre, Golf del Sur ☎ 922 73 82 15 🕐 Daily 9am–midnight 🚌 TITSA buses 115, 470, 484

ESPAÑA €

Pollo mojo (garlic chicken) is the favourite at this non-smoking restaurant.

✚ D7 ✉ Calle Grande, Adeje ☎ 923 71 00 02 🕐 Sat–Thu lunch, dinner 🚌 TITSA bus 473

FONDA CENTRAL €€

Dine in the covered courtyard of a fine old Canarian building (now a hotel), on grilled fresh fish, prawns and several versions of chicken.

✚ D7 ✉ Calle Grande, Adeje ☎ 922 78 15 50 🕐 Lunch, dinner daily 🚌 TITSA bus 473

EL INTI €€

Popular restaurant specializing in Peruvian fare, live Andian music Thursday evenings.

✚ F9 ✉ Trasera CC San Blas, Golf del Sur ☎ 922 73 83 26 🕐 Sat–Thu 6.30pm–midnight 🚌 TITSA bus 470, 483

EL JABLE €€

Appealing bar-restaurant in an untouristy village near the Médano exit of the motorway, serving tasty local dishes.

WHERE TO EAT

Most places are simply called restaurants, making choices simpler here than on the continent. Local Canarian establishments usually offer everything from a light meal of tapas (usually called *entradas*), a sandwich or salad to a full hot meal. Canarians are casual about what they serve when, happily serving a selection of starters without a main course in the evening–although more formal restaurants may be less flexible.

✚ F8 ✉ Calle Bentejui 9, San Isidro ☎ 922 39 06 98 🕐 Mon 7.30–11, Tue–Sat 1–4, 7.30–11 🚌 TITSA bus 111

MIRABELLO RESTAURANTE €–€€

German and Austrian cuisine; the beer garden has barbeque with live music on Sundays.

✚ F8 ✉ Calle Bethencourt Alfonso 74, San Miguel ☎ 922 70 06 27 🕐 Mon, Tue, Fri 6pm–midnight, Sat–Sun 11am–midnight 🚌 TITSA bus 342

OTELO €–€€

The two-level terrace overhangs the ravine at Barranco del Infierno, and the garlic chicken and braised rabbit are as good as the view.

✚ D7 ✉ El Molino, Adeje ☎ 922 78 03 74 🕐 Lunch, dinner daily 🚌 TITSA bus 473

TASQUITA PIMENTON €€

In a meticulously restored village home, the chef serves exceptional *pimientos padron* and dishes using local produce and cheeses.

✚ G7 ✉ Plaza de La Luz, Arico el Nuevo ☎ 922 76 84 86 🕐 Wed–Sun 1–11 🚌 TITSA bus 130

EL TERRERO €€

Tasty traditional dishes in a fine old home.

✚ F7 ✉ Calle Iglesia 1, Granadilla de Abona ☎ 922 77 02 00 🕐 Daily 6.30–10pm 🚌 TITSA buses 470, 416

One of the smallest Canary Islands, La Gomera covers only 372sq km (145sq miles). Steep ravines between settlements led Gomerians to develop a communication method of whistled sounds that can be understood 2.5km (1.5 miles) away.

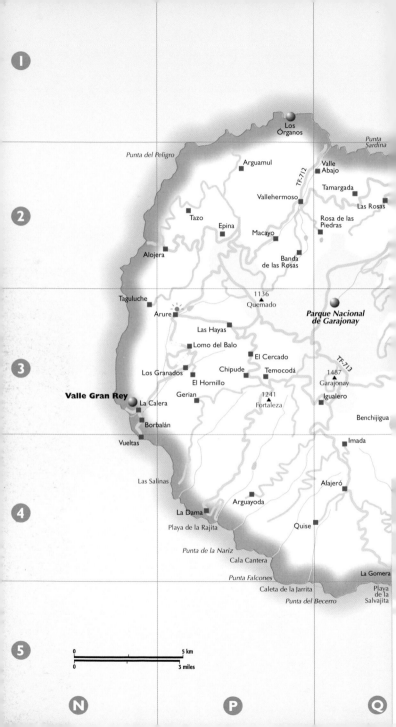

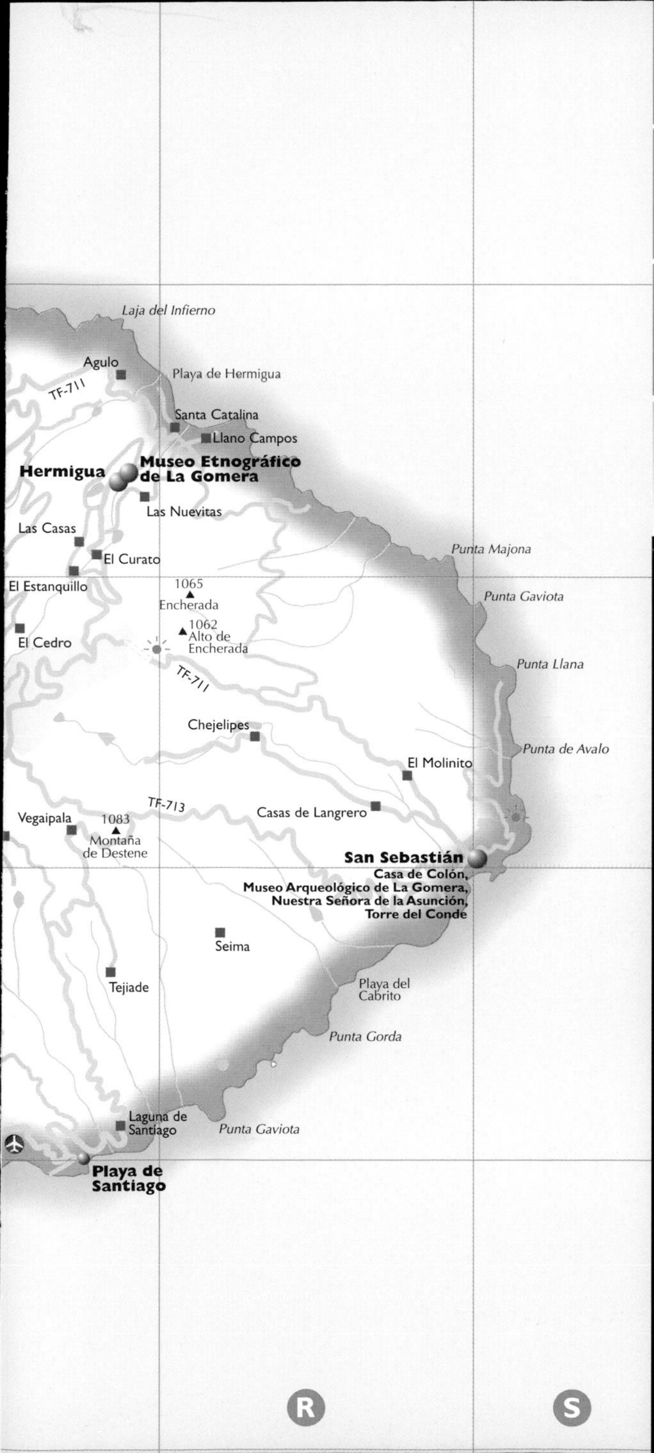

Laja del Infierno

Agulo

Playa de Hermigua

TF-711

Santa Catalina

Llano Campos

Hermigua
Museo Etnográfico
de La Gomera

Las Nuevitas

Las Casas

El Curato

Punta Majona

El Estanquillo

1065
▲
Encherada

Punta Gaviota

El Cedro

1062
▲ Alto de
Encherada

Punta Llana

TF-711

Chejelipes

Punta de Avalo

El Molinito

TF-713

Casas de Langrero

Vegaipala

1083
▲
Montaña
de Destene

San Sebastián
Casa de Colón,
Museo Arqueológico de La Gomera,
Nuestra Señora de la Asunción,
Torre del Conde

Seima

Tejiade

Playa del
Cabrito

Punta Gorda

Laguna de
Santiago

Punta Gaviota

Playa de
Santiago

R   S

Parque Nacional de Garajonay

TOP
25

HIGHLIGHTS

- Mirador Los Roques
- Mirador de Vallehermoso
- Walk in the laurel forest
- Drive along the spectacu-
lar road through the park
(▷ 104)

TIPS

- Drive round the island
clockwise. For the most part
this will keep you on the
inside of the sharp curves
with long, steep drop-offs.
- Drive down into Playa
Santiago and Playa Gran Rey.

**La Gomera, rising abruptly from the
Atlantic with few places flat enough
to afford a foothold, is crowned by
Garajonay National Park. The 3,984ha
(9,844 acres) of the world's largest
pre-glacial forest is a UNESCO World
Heritage Site.**

Ancient forest Remarkable for the 70 per cent
of its area that is covered by a dense laurel forest, similar to those that covered Europe in the
Tertiary period, the park, comprising much of the
top of the island, is a naturalist's dream, home to
many plants and animals that are indigenous to
this island. La Gomera's streams and springs are
fed by clouds and by the mists that often circle
its highest peaks, all of which lie within the park
boundaries. All land travel between different parts

Lush vegetation and rounded peaks are features of the national park (left); idyllic woodland scene (middle); hikers should come prepared with warm and waterproof gear (right)

of the island must pass through it. Narrow side roads drop from the lush natural forest down the *barrancos* (steep ravines) to towns and villages by the sea.

Rewarding walking Hiking trips in the park and surrounding *barrancos* are, for many, the highlight of their trip, with luggage transfer and bus or taxi pick-up easy to arrange. Trekking in this steep terrain is a challenge, but the paths through moss-draped forests that open to breathtaking vertical views are unmatched anywhere. Hikers certainly need to be fit, since the terrain goes up and down, and the altitude in the park climbs up to 1,487m (4,879ft). Since many of the treks are down a *barranco* to a destination at the bottom, most hikers prefer to be let off at the top and met at the bottom.

THE BASICS

➕ Q3

✉ Centro de Visitante, Juego de Bolas, La Palmita

☎ 922 80 09 93

🕐 Daily 9:30–4:30

🍴 La Laguna Grande (€€–€€€)

🚌 Bus 1 traverses park but does not reach visitor centre

♿ Few

💷 Free

❓ Free guided tours every Sat, more often in summer; advance booking required

San Sebastián

HIGHLIGHTS

● Torre del Conde
● Iglesia de la Asunción
● Playa de San Sebastián
● Casa de Agunada and Pozo del Aguada (well)

TIPS

● The ferry terminal is 1.5km (1 mile) from the centre, where all sights are conveniently close together.
● San Sebastián is a perfect base for exploring, with good bus connections to the whole island.

Capital and chief city of the island, laid-back San Sebastián was where Christopher Columbus outfitted the *Santa Maria*, *Pinta* and *Niña* for their momentous voyage to the New World.

Town layout Hemmed in by the towering mountains, the city faces the bay with a long public beach and a trio of attractive parks. The commercial centre and residential streets behind them have little flat space before they begin climbing up the steep hillside above. On one side a cliff towers over the maritime station, with a parador on top. A tunnel beneath allows access to Playa de la Cueva. Opposite, the seaside Avenida de los Descubridores borders Playa San Sebastián, the island's longest sand beach, ending abruptly at the foot of another cliff.

Clockwise from far left: Plaza de las Américas; dragon tree in the parador courtyard; schooner moored in the harbour; the drawing room of the parador is filled with period furniture; houses painted in bright and cheerful colours; looking down on the harbour

Old town The small Plaza de la Constitución is shaded by huge trees that shade benches and a spaceship-shaped café. It adjoins the larger paved Plaza de las Américas, the centre of community life (and a place for impromptu football games in the evening), with cafés and palms. Between these parks, Calle Real was the town's original street and the old Customs House, Casa de la Agunada, is at the site where legend holds that Columbus filled casks with water for his voyage.

Columbian era Parque de la Torre's gardens surround the only intact relic of the Columbian period, the stone Torre del Conde, built by Hernán Peraza, between 1445 and 1447. Casa Colón, Nuestra Señora de la Asunción and the Ermita de San Sebastián stand among Calle Real's 18th- and 19th-century houses.

THE BASICS

🚩 S4

🍴 Plentiful

🚌 Bus (*guagua*) from station on Calle Colón to all parts of island

⛴ From Los Cristianos on Tenerife

ℹ Calle Real 4, tel 922 14 15 12; Mon–Sat 9–1.30, 3.30–6

More to See

HERMIGUA

The small city has nice architecture and well-kept coloured façades, especially around the Ayuntamiento and Jacarandas hotel. A small *gofio* mill museum and El Convento Artisanania are worth stops. There is a small, pleasant beach at Playa Caleta.

➕ Q2 ✉ TF 711 🍴 Several 🚌 Bus 2 from San Sebastián ♿ Few

HERMIGUA: MUSEO ETNOGRÁFICO DE LA GOMERA

Two floors of exhibits show the adaptation of people to the demands of the island, interpreting fishing, forestry, agriculture and the tools used, plus special exhibits on textiles and wine making.

➕ Q2 ✉ Carretera General de las Hoyeas 99 ☎ 922 88 19 60 🕐 Tue–Fri 10–6, Sat–Sun 10–2 🍴 Café (€–€€) 🚌 Bus 2 ♿ Few 💷 Inexpensive

LOS ÓRGANOS

Huge basaltic columns fall nearly 100m (330ft) into the sea, a spectacular sight visible only from the water. Whale and sightseeing cruises often include this in their itineraries, (▷ 105).

➕ P1 ✉ Northwest coast

PLAYA DE SANTIAGO

Plunging along the side of the cliffs, through a canyon of white-washed houses one reaches the little town stretched along Avenida Maritima, facing the narrow cobble beach. Huge columnar basalt cliffs loom behind the town. Stop to see the gardens at the Tecina Golf Course (18 holes and the only course on the island) and Hotel Tecina, on the way into town.

➕ Q5 🍴 Along Avenida Maritima 🚌 Bus 3 from San Sebastián ♿ Few ℹ Edificio Las Vistas 8, tel 922 80 54 58; Mon–Sat 9–1, 4–6

SAN SEBASTIÁN: CASA DE COLÓN

Built in the 17th century, some sources say on the site of the house where Columbus was a

The organ pipes of Los Órganos

Boats in the harbour at Playa de Santiago

guest, but there is no record of this. Now it is a museum of his route and pre-Columbian South American pottery.

🔝 S4 ✉ 56 Calle Real ☎ 922 14 15 12 🕐 Mon–Fri 10–1, 4–6.30 🍴 Nearby ♿ None ✋ Free

SAN SEBASTIÁN: MUSEO ARQUEOLÓGICO DE LA GOMERA

The staff of this living museum are actively involved in archaeology, exploring the history of the island and people, especially its original inhabitants.

🔝 S4 ✉ Calle Torres Padilla 8 ☎ 922 14 15 86 🕐 Jun–Sep Mon–Fri 10–7, Sat–Sun 10–2; Oct–May Mon–Fri 10–6, Sat–Sun 10–2 🍴 Nearby ♿ None ✋ Free

SAN SEBASTIÁN: NUESTRA SEÑORA DE LA ASUNCIÓN

The present church was erected in the 17th century, a fine example of local adaptation of Gothic and baroque styles. Hand-carved wooden altars are a highlight, as is a mural celebrating the defeat of a British naval squadron in 1743. An arch to the left of the entrance is called Puerta del Perdón because aboriginal Guanches were said to have been massacred after passing through it.

🔝 S4 ✉ Calle Real 🕐 Before morning and evening Mass 🍴 Nearby ♿ Few ✋ Free

SAN SEBASTIÁN: TORRE DEL CONDE

Construction of this defensive fortification began in 1450, shortly after the start of the Spanish conquest, with the tower being finally completed in 1477. In 1488 the hated governor Hernán Peraza was killed in an uprising and his wife barricaded herself in this tower until she was rescued. The only known structure in San Sebastián from Columbus' time, it now houses a museum with maps and documents.

🔝 S4 ✉ Parque de la Torre 🕐 Mon–Fri 10–1 🍴 Nearby ♿ None ✋ Free

The church of Nuestra Señora de la Asunción in San Sebastián

Torre del Conde, San Sebastián

San Sebastián

Follow in the footsteps of Christopher Columbus to explore a small city that still has the air of a colonial port little changed by tourism.

DISTANCE: 2km (1.2 miles) **ALLOW:** 2 hours, with stops

START

PASEO FRED OLSEN
✚ S4

END

AVENIDA DE LOS DESCUBRIDORES
✚ S4

LA GOMERA WALK

1 Begin at the marina, under the high cliff overlooking the harbour, and turn right at the broad, palm-fringed Plaza de las Américas.

2 Walk past the arcaded Ayuntamiento (town hall) and cross the street for a better look at the carved wooden balconies and clock tower of this elegant building.

3 Continue along Calle Virgin de Guadeloupe, turning left to cross Plaza de la Constitución, shaded by huge trees. The old Customs House on the right contains the tourist office. In its courtyard is Pozo de la Aguada, the well where Columbus is believed to have drawn water for his ships.

4 Turn right on leaving the Customs House and walk up Calle Real, lined with brightly painted stucco buildings and elegant old mansions, to Nuestra Señora de la Asunción.

8 Through the gate at the opposite end of the garden is Avenida de los Descubridores, bordering the sandy beach of Playa de San Sebastián.

7 A right turn onto Avenida de Colón and a left on Calle Fernandez lead directly into the green gardens of Parque de la Torre. Here stands the oldest intact building on the island, Torre del Conde (▷ 101).

6 Just past Casa de Colón is the little chapel Ermita de San Sebastián, built in 1540. Turn left, following Calle San Sebastián to Calle Ruis de Padron and turn left again.

5 Beyond, on the right, Casa Colón (▷ 100) is now a museum of the discoveries. Among these historic sights are attractive shops and galleries.

Parque Nacional de Garajonay

This drive throws into sharp relief the contrast between the lush forest of the national park and the barren *barrancos* below.

DISTANCE: 30km (19 miles)   **ALLOW:** 2 hours, with stops

START

TF713 AT INTERSECTION WITH PLAYA SANTIAGO ROAD
✚ Q3

1 Enter the protected natural reserve and the landscape changes from high gorse-grown moors to green cedars, pines and hardwoods. Graceful ferns and wildflowers grow underneath.

2 As the road continues through a thick cedar forest hemming each side like hedgerows, watch for the right turn to the tiny chapel of Ermita las Nieves.

3 Huge domes of rock tower ahead, with miradors for viewing Roque Agando and neighbouring roques. Signs explain that these are cores and vents of ancient volcanoes, exposed as the cones eroded away.

4 At Mirador Tajaque, on the left, signage tells how the eons of erosion by streams of water from the mist-shrouded laurel forests have carved these deep *barrancos*, leaving sharp spines between them.

END

VALLE GRAN REY/VALLEHERMOSA ROAD INTERSECTION
✚ P3

7 In 7km (4.5 miles) the road forks. To the left is Valle de Gran Rey, to the right Vallehermosa. Either road leaves the park shortly, dropping steeply down into green valleys.

6 La Laguna Grande, a recreation complex (daily 10–4) with swimming, picnicking and restaurants, lies at the intersection with a narrow road through the thick forest to the north. At this site, ancient witches were believed to hold rituals in the full of the moon.

5 Drive along the narrow knife-edge of Cumbre de Tajaque, only as wide as the road itself, and dropping sharply on both sides. When another road to Playa Santiago drops off to the left, stay to the right, along the northern flank of Mount Garajonay.

Shopping

ARTESANIA SANTA ANA
Varied crafts and local specialty foods such as *mojo* sauce, fig biscuits and palm honey are all available to buy here and make ideal souvenirs.

S4 ✉ Calle Real 41, San Sebastián ☎ 922 14 18 64 🚌 Walk from ferry

CENTRO DE VISITANTES
From Tuesdays to Fridays, artisans demonstrate their traditional crafts including weaving, pottery, woodworking and basket making. Their work is then sold in the shop.

✚ Q2 ✉ Juego de Bolas, Las Rosas ☎ 922 80 09 93 🚌 Bus 2 to Las Rosas

CHIPUDE
The town of Chipude and its outlying villages are well-known for their beautiful pottery, made in the traditional way without a wheel, from clay, sand and red ochre. Buy it directly from the craftsmen, who display it outside their homes.

✚ P3 ✉ Chipude, Pavon and El Cercado 🚌 Bus 4

SAN SEBASTIÁN MARKET
Early in the morning vendors including fishermen, local farmers, palm honey makers and others gather in the market building in San Sebastián. It is a low-key but friendly and brightly decorated place, and offers a good source of food souvenirs, with the added satisfaction of buying directly from the producers.

✚ S4 ✉ Next to the bus station, San Sebastián ⏰ Tue–Sat 7–1

Entertainment and Activities

GOMERA DIVE RESORT
www.gomera-dive-resort.com
This company provides PADI diving courses for all levels of ability in the sheltered harbour of Valle Gran Rey.

✚ N3 ✉ Vueltas, Valle Gran Rey ☎ 619 91 66 82 🚌 Bus 1

MACONDO
This combo beach bar/restaurant (with a menu of seafood, pasta and drinks) is a good headquarters for beachgoers, with a shower, deckchairs and sunshades to hire and other useful things.

✚ R2 ✉ Playa de la Caleta, 6km (4 miles) from Hermigua ⏰ Daily from 11am 🚌 Bus 2

LA TASCA BAR
www.barlatasca.com
Lively bar with live music, on the walking street in the Vueltas part of town.

✚ N3 ✉ Calle Abisinia 5, Valle Gran Rey ☎ 649 89

MIEL DE PALMA
La Gomera produces an unusual palm honey, which is not honey at all. Locally called *guarapo*, it is actually made from the sap of the indigenous palm tree, *Phoenix canariensis*. It is used to sweeten pastries and is also made into a liqueur. Bottled in small, sturdy jars, Miel de Palma makes a gift unique to the island.

33 16 ⏰ Tue–Sun 8pm–midnight 🚌 Bus 1

TINA EXCURSIONES
www.excursiones-tina.com
Whale watching for common, spotted, rough toothed, bottle nosed dolphins, pilot, sperm and Bryde's whales, plus excursions to see the organ-pipe basalt cliffs of Los Órganos. Trips are 3 hours to all-day. Some include swimming and fresh grilled tuna lunch.

✚ N3 ✉ Apartado 16, Valle Gran Rey ☎ 922 80 58 85 ⏰ Cruises: Mon 10am Playa de Santiago; Tue–Fri, Sun 10.45 Valle Gran Rey 🍴 Bar, snacks on board 🚌 Bus 1 💰 Expensive

Restaurants

PRICES

Prices are approximate, based on a 3-course meal for one person.

€€€   over €40
€€   €20–€40
€   under €20

CASA CONCHITA €

Casa Conchita offers traditional Canarian *carne fiesta* (stew) and sea-food. The dessert house special is banana with Gomerian palm honey. This plain little restaurant is one book you can't judge by its cover—the food is delicious.
➕ P3   ✉ Arure   🕐 Daily lunch, dinner

CASTILLO DEL MAR €€–€€€

www.castillo-del-mar.com
Now a stylish bar and restaurant, this 19th-century fort has views of Teide on Tenerife. Brunch is served on the second and fourth Sundays of the month, and there is a market on the first and third Sundays.
➕ P2   ✉ Parque Marítimo, Vallehermoso   ☎ 922 80 04 97   🕐 Thu–Mon 11am–sunset   🚌 Bus shuttle Fri from Valle Gran Rey

CHARCO DEL CONDE €€

Specializes in fresh fish and Canarian dishes.
➕ Q5   ✉ Avenida Maritima, Playa de Santiago   ☎ 922 80 54 03   🕐 Mon–Sat 9–10   🚌 Bus 3

CUATRO CAMINOS €€

A typical menu, but usually well prepared and served in a pleasant setting.
➕ S4   ✉ Calle Ruiz de Padron 36, San Sebastián   ☎ 922 14 12 60   🕐 Mon–Sat

LAGUNA GRANDE €€–€€€

www.laguna-grande.es
The specialties, served at this restaurant in the middle of the national park, include the *potaje de berros* (watercress soup), grilled meats and fresh fish.
➕ Q3   ✉ TF713, Garonjay National Park   ☎ 922 69 70 70, 699 44 54 17   🕐 Lunch, dinner   🚌 TITSA bus 1

LA PALMITA €€

Choose the Gran Parrilla—a wonderful feast of grilled meats—and La Gomera wines.

FAMED FOR CHEESE

Gomeran cheese is made with milk from three local breeds of sheep, usually blended with goat milk, which adds buttery richness. The cheeses may be eaten young, fresh, and soft, while they have a nuanced, mild flavour, but most often they are aged until their interior is dense and brittle, tasting of the flowers and herbs the grazing goats ate while producing milk. Smoked versions have a more pungent flavour.

➕ S4   ✉ 300m (330yd) from the visitor center, Agulo   ☎ 922 80 09 78, 626 38 63 39   🕐 Daily 10–10   🚌 Bus 2

EL PARAISO €€

Rabbit and goat are on the menu and desserts are made in-house.
➕ N3   ✉ Avenida Marítima 4, Valle Gran Rey   ☎ 922 80 50 42   🕐 Sun–Fri 12–11   🚌 Bus 1

EL PEJIN €–€€

Choose your fresh fish from the case in front or take the chef's advice on that day's catch, perhaps dorado or *boca negro*. The portions are generous and the family owners congenial.
➕ S4   ✉ Calle Real 14, San Sebastián   🕐 Lunch, dinner

RESTAURANTE JUNONIA €–€€

This friendly, harbour-facing restaurant specializes in Canarian dishes and fresh fish served with *papas arrugadas*.
➕ Q5   ✉ Avenida Martima, Playa de Santiago   ☎ 922 89 54 50   🕐 Wed–Mon lunch, dinner   🚌 Bus 3

TERRAZA EL MIRADOR LA CALERA €€–€€€

www.restauranteslagomera.com
Dine above the town of La Calera, on Gomerian specialties and fish.
➕ N3   ✉ La Gurona 13, Valle Gran Rey   ☎ 922 80 50 86   🕐 Fri–Wed 12–11.30 (10.30 in winter)   🚌 Bus 1

While the popular image of Tenerife's shore lined with rows of sun-splashed holiday apartments and holiday complexes is certainly true in the resort areas, the choice of lodging on the island is far more wide-ranging.

Where to Stay

Introduction

You will find lodging at all levels in Tenerife, from modest *hotel rurales* in small towns to smart city hotels and elegant five-star resort complexes. You'll also find all styles, from brand-new steel-and-glass hotels to traditional buildings with balconies overlooking palm-filled patios.

Booking Ahead

It's a puzzle for all travellers: should you book ahead and be locked into a week at a hotel sight-unseen? Or should you reserve the first night or two and look around for a place of your choice? If a week in the warm sun is your dream, it is probably better to book ahead and stay in the same place. But if you plan to drive around the island and see the sights, as long as you avoid the busy holiday seasons, you should not have trouble finding interesting places to stay. Booking ahead is easy, either through the hotel's own website, by phone or fax, or through one of the many booking services that specializes in island properties.

It's Not All Resorts

Tenerife offers many different lodging options. Those who wish to be close to nightlife will prefer the popular hotels and apartments of the coastal resorts. Those travelling with children should scour hotel websites to find play facilities, special pools and entertainment programmes. Visitors who plan to hire a car and tour the island might choose character-filled hotels such as Hotel Rural Senderos de Abona, in a restored 19th-century mansion in the hill town of Granadilla, or an apartment in the hillside farm, Finca Vista Bonita, in San Miguel.

MONEY SAVERS
● Prices are usually lower for stays of five days or longer.
● Rates within the same hotel usually vary with ocean or mountain (or no) view.
● August and December (up to 7 Jan) tend to be the most expensive months, corresponding to Spanish holiday seasons.

From top: Arona Gran Hotel, Los Cristianos; Parador, Teide; hotel pool; Puerto de la Cruz

Budget Hotels

ACUARIO

www.tenerifehotelacuario.com
The helpful staff, quiet surroundings and well-kept swimming pool on a terrace overlooking the city compensate for the 25-minute walk to Plaza del Charco. Internet, lounge areas and parking are added bonuses.
✚ F3 ✉ Parque de las Flores 35, Puerto de la Cruz ☎ 922 37 41 42 🚌 TITSA buses 102 and 340 from the airport

APARTHOTEL NEPTUNO

www.aparthotelneptuno.com
Attractive apartment complex on the south coast near Playa Fañabé has three pools, a restaurant, bar, gym, playgrounds and 24-hour concierge.
✚ D8 ✉ Calle Cataluna 3 (Torviscas), Costa Adeje ☎ 922 71 30 78 🚌 Own bus to Los Cristianos, Adeje

BIKERS INN

Inexpensive lodging close to the ferry landing, and they rent bikes as well.
✚ N3 ✉ Calle San Miguel 1, Valle Gran Rey, La Gomera ☎ 922 80 51 42 🚌 Bus 1 from San Sebastián

FINCA VISTA BONITA

www.finca-vistabonita.com
Sitting on the flank of the mountain above San Miguel, the *finca* has 13 fully equipped apartments with free internet and satellite TV, as well as balconies overlooking the hotel's gardens, farmland and the sea. A good choice for summer, only 13km (8 miles) from the beach, but high enough to catch cooling breezes.
✚ F8 ✉ Calle El Portillo, San Miguel de Abona ☎ 922 71 29 28 🚌 TITSA bus 342

HOTEL GARAJONAY

The budget cousin of Hotel Torre del Conde, which it adjoins, this no-frills hotel offers 29 rooms right in the centre of town, overlooking the main street and the park. The two hotels share the friendly staff.
✚ S4 ✉ Calle Ruiz de Padron 17, San Sebastián, La Gomera ☎ 922 87 05 50 🚌 Less than 1km (0.5 miles) from ferry landing, near the bus station

HOTEL GEMA PUERTO

www.gemahoteles.com
Comfortable, small (48-room) hotel in the centre of the city and walking distance to all attractions. An internet café is off the lobby, reserved for hotel guests after 8pm.
✚ F3 ✉ Calle Blanco 13, Puerto de la Cruz ☎ 922 37 40 49 🚌 TITSA buses 102 and 340 from the airport

HOTEL PUERTO AZUL

www.puerto-azul.com
Small, unpretentious 26-room hotel, only a few minutes' walk from the Plaza Charco and the bus station; some rooms have terraces with views of Mount Teide.
✚ F3 ✉ Calle Lomo 24, Puerto de La Cruz ☎ 922 38 32 13 🚌 TITSA buses 102 and 340 from the airport

LOS TELARES

www.apartamentosgomera.com
A traditional home with 28 guest suites (each with a kitchen), part of a group of rural apartments and houses high in the Garajonay National Forest, in the town of Hermigua and on the seaside. Well appointed, comfortable accommodations with privacy and access to local culture and environment.
✚ Q2 ✉ Carretera General 10, Hermigua, La Gomera ☎ 922 88 07 81 🚌 Bus 2 from San Sebastián

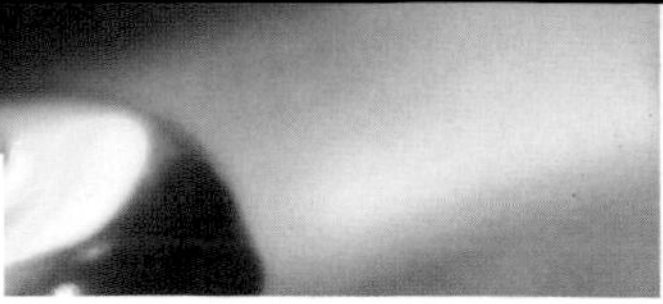

Mid-Range Hotels

PRICES

Expect to pay between €75 and €150 per night for a double room in a mid-range hotel.

APARTAMENTOS TAPAHUGA

www.tapahuga.com

Attractive wooden balconies overlook the fishing harbour. The 29 comfortable and well decorated apartments have full kitchens, and guests can enjoy the pool and sundeck on the roof, and an interior patio.

Q5 Avenida Marítima, Playa de Santiago 922 89 51 59 Bus 3 from San Sebastián

GRAN HOTEL TURQUESA PLAYA

www.hotelturquesa.com

Close to the bus station and Playa Jardín, with 350 well-decorated rooms with terraces and refrigerators, the Turquesa offers all the four-star amenities, including four restaurants, four pools and sports facilities.

F3 Calle Antonio Ruiz Álvarez 7, Urbanización Turquesa Playa, Puerto de la Cruz 922 37 13 08 TITSA buses 102 and 340 from the airport

HOTEL FONDA CENTRAL

The historic coaching inn is set in a traditional Canarian building, with carved wooden balconies overlooking the quiet central patios. But there are mod cons, too—such as internet access in all rooms. The restaurant (▷ 90) serves local dishes.

D7 Calle Grande 26, Adeje 922 78 15 50 TITSA bus 473 from Los Cristianos

HOTEL GRAN REY

www.hotel-granrey.com

Only 40m (45yd) from the sea, this is a resort hotel with dining and concierge services. Tennis, organised hiking, walking and cycling tours, paragliding and diving can be arranged. Each of the 99 rooms has a terrace.

N3 Apartados de Correos 24, Valle Gran Rey, La Gomera 922 80 58 59 Bus 1 from San Sebastián

EL NAVIO HOTEL RURAL

Secluded in the middle of a vast banana plantation that was the south coast's first, the descendants of the hotel's founder have created a charming oasis of rooms with large terraces overlooking ocean sunsets. Sample local cuisine here, with fruits and vegetables from their own gardens, and savour an experience far removed from the nearby resorts.

www.elnavio.net

C6 Avenida de los Pescadores, Alcalá 922 86 56 80 TITSA buses 473, 477

HOTEL MARQUESA

www.hotelmarquesa.com

Located right off the Plaza Charco and Paseo San Telmo, close to the main bus station, this is a pleasant 144-room hotel in a historic building (1712) in the centre of city life, close to all attractions and dining.

F3 Calle Quintana 11, Puerto de la Cruz 922 38 31 51 TITSA buses 102 and 340 from the airport

HOTEL OASIS OROTAVA PALACE

www.hotelesoasis.com

Large 225-room luxury hotel in the middle of the city. Large pool, hydro-massage, fully wheelchair-accessible, restaurant, café and terrace with Jacuzzi.

F3 Calle Aguilar y Quesada 3, Puerto de la Cruz 922 36 88 60 TITSA buses 102 and 340 from the airport

HOTEL PELINOR

www.hotelpelinor.com

In the heart of the city, a few steps from Plaza de la Candelaria, the 73-room Pelinor is good value for money.

d3 Calle Bethencourt Alfonso 8, Santa Cruz 922 24 68 75 Tranvia 'Guimera'

HOTEL RURAL SENDEROS DE ABONA

www.senderosdeabona.com

A local family has restored this gracious 1856 mansion into an inn, with 17 rooms

furnished with antiques, but with modern bathrooms. Plant-filled patios, balconies, gardens, a good dining room and even a small museum are extra attractions.

➕ F7 ✉ Calle Iglesia 1, Granadilla de Abona ☎ 922 77 02 00 🚌 TITSA bus 130 from Santa Cruz, 470 from Los Cristianos

HOTEL RURAL TAMAHUCHE

www.ecoturismocanarias.com/hoteltamahuche
The 10 rooms in this 1896 home have direct access to patios and gardens. The inn is dedicated to sustainable tourism, clean energy, recycling and serving local products at breakfast (included in room rate).

➕ P2 ✉ La Hoya 20, Vallehermoso, La Gomera ☎ 922 80 11 76 🚌 Bus 2, 4 from San Sebastián

HOTEL RURAL VICTORIA

www.hotelruralvictoria.com
This delightful small hotel in a 16th-century mansion is full service, with a well-known dining room, internet, satellite TV, bar and sundeck.

➕ G4 ✉ Hermano Apolinar 8, La Orotava ☎ 922 33 16 83 🚌 TITSA buses 101, 107, 108 345, 347, 348

HOTEL TENERIFE PLAYA

www.h10hotels.es
Large in-town hotel 50m (55yd) from the sea and Lago Martiánez, close to all major attractions and dining in the city. There are 324 rooms.

➕ F3 ✉ Avenida de Colón 12, Puerto de la Cruz ☎ 922 38 22 11 🚌 TITSA buses 102 and 340 from the airport

HOTEL TORRE DEL CONDE

www.hoteltorredelconde.com
The roof terrace and many of the 38 rooms overlook the park and the oldest building on the island, the Torre del Conde, where Columbus visited. Free wireless internet.

➕ S4 ✉ Calle Ruiz de Padrón 19, San Sebastián, La Gomera ☎ 922 87 00 00 🚶 Less than 1km (0.5 miles) from ferry landing, near the bus station

PARADOR DE CAÑADAS DEL TEIDE

www.parador.es
A more spectacular setting would be hard to imagine, inside the national park and centrally located to all park sites. Spain's highest mountain, Teide, towers across the volcanic floor of the park. Comfortable with all of the expected amenities of a Parador, including a full restaurant, snack bar and bar. Walking and hiking trails are all around, Los Roques de Garcia are within minutes of the door.

➕ E6 ✉ TF21 at Las Cañadas, Teide National Park ☎ 922 37 48 41 🚌 TITSA buses 342, 348

PARQUE TAJINASTE

www.parque-tajinaste.com
Aparthotel with 80 studio or larger apartments with full kitchens, private baths and terraces/gardens, located right by the botanic gardens. Bungalows are also available on site.

➕ F3 ✉ Calle Retama 4, Puerto de la Cruz ☎ 922 38 46 52 🚌 TITSA buses 102 and 340 from the airport, 101 or 107 from city centre

TIGAIGA TENERIFE

www.tigaiga.com
High on a hill over the city centre, the 83-room hotel is surrounded by beautiful gardens and adjoins Taoro Park, a leafy place favoured by runners. Spacious rooms have thoughtful details—bathrobes, make-up mirrors and fresh flowers.

➕ F3 ✉ Parque Taoro 28, Puerto de la Cruz ☎ 922 38 35 00 🚌 TITSA buses 102 and 340 from the airport

APARTMENTS

Apartments (and budget hotels) often do not include toiletries such as soap and shampoo. The kitchen will likely have soap, but rarely basics such as salt and pepper. Small packets of those, as well as sugar and tea, can save buying large quantities to leave behind. Most apartment complexes have nearby or on-site grocery stores, so provisioning is easy.

Luxury Hotels

PRICES

Expect to pay more than €150 per night for a double room in a luxury hotel.

ARONA GRAN HOTEL

www.aronahotel.com
Overlooking the sea and beach, the Arona Gran Hotel is built in stepped-back layers that ensure that all of its 391 rooms and 12 junior suites have a private terrace. The three pools are heated in winter and overlook the sea.

➕ D8 ✉ Avenida Juan Carlos I 38, Los Cristianos ☎ 922 75 06 78 🚌 TITSA bus 111 or 487 from airport; bus 110 or 111 from Santa Cruz. Free airport transfer for 7-night stays

ATLANTIDA SANTA CRUZ

www.hoteles-silken.com
A thoroughly modern high-rise hotel near Parque Marítimo and the Auditorio, the Atlantida's 144 state-of-the-art rooms include 25 junior suites. The glass-and-steel tower is a striking landmark on the city skyline, and the wide views from its lush rooftop pool and terrace stretch across the city to the Anaga mountains and to Mount Teide itself.

➕ b5 (fold-out map) ✉ Avenida Tres de Mayo, Santa Cruz ☎ 922 29 45 00 🚌 Central bus/Tranvia station

CLEOPATRA PALACE HOTEL

www.expogrupo.com
In a prime beachfront setting on the promenade at Playa del Camisón, the Cleopatra is one of several hotels in the enormous Mare Nostrum complex, all of which are hard to miss with their over-the-top theme-park architecture. Brightly decorated rooms all have balconies and 24-hour room service; suites have their own private pools.

➕ D8 ✉ Avenida de las Américas, Playa de las Américas ☎ 922 75 75 45 🚌 TITSA buses 342, 416, 417, 450, 467, 472, 477, 483, 488

GRAN HOTEL BAHÍA DEL DUQUE RESORT

www.bahia-duque.com
Bringing Tenerife lodgings to a new level, the 480

OASIS FOR ART-LOVERS

Spacious, genteel and filled with 19th-century Canarian art, the up-scale 250-room Hotel Botanico is near the botanic gardens and has a palm-shaded poolside area and a 18-hole putting green. It's an updated look at the Tenerife that Agatha Christie knew and loved.
www.hotelbotanico.com
➕ F3 ✉ Avenida Richard Yeoward 1, Puerto de la Cruz ☎ 922 38 14 00 🚌 TITSA buses 102 and 340 from the airport

guest rooms and suites here are spread among 21 buildings that cluster around a faux village plaza. The extensive grounds are manicured, the beach is well furnished and served by attentive staff, and a full array of up-market dining and shopping options are on or close to the compound.

➕ D8 ✉ Avenida Bruselas, Costa Adeje ☎ 922 74 69 00 🚌 TITSA bus 111 connects to the airport

HOTEL JARDÍN TECINA

www.jardin-tecina.com
This flashy resort hotel boasts multiple pools, a spa, and 18 holes of golf on a cliff-top overlooking the sea. The resort sits above the town and is architecturally designed to look like a Gomeran village.

➕ Q5 ✉ Playa de Santiago, La Gomera ☎ 922 14 58 50, Reservations 902 22 21 40 🚌 Bus 3 from San Sebastián

PARADOR CONDE DE LA GOMERA

www.parador.es
The clifftop setting, views of Mount Teide across the sea and antique furnishings and décor make up for the dour staff at this 58-room member of Spain's Parador system.

➕ S4 ✉ Llano de la Horca 1, San Sebastián, La Gomera ☎ 922 87 11 00 🚌 Taxi or stiff climb from the ferry landing below

Need to Know

Use this section to help plan your visit to Tenerife. Here is advice on planning your visit, travelling to the island and getting around, along with useful information on the practical aspects of your stay.

Planning Ahead

When to Go

Tenerife is popular with European travellers for its year-round sunny, warm climate. Not surprisingly, it is most crowded during the winter, when northerners come to escape the cold, during the traditional Spanish holiday periods of August and December, and during Carnival in February.

TIME

L Tenerife is on GMT, like the UK. Summertime (GMT+1) operates from late March to late October.

AVERAGE DAILY MAXIMUM TEMPERATURES

JAN	FEB	MAR	APR	MAY	JUN	JUL	AUG	SEP	OCT	NOV	DEC
20°C	21°C	23°C	24°C	25°C	27°C	28°C	29°C	28°C	26°C	23°C	20°C
68°F	70°F	73°F	75°F	77°F	81°F	82°F	84°F	82°F	79°F	73°F	68°F

Spring (March–June) is marked by mild temperatures and mostly sunny, possible rain in the north. For weather, the best time of the year to visit.
Summer (July–September) is the hottest period but still comfortable and dry. Temperatures can reach 35°C (95°F). The coolest part of the island is the north.
Autumn (October–December) is a transition period. Summer temperatures prevail in September but moderate in mid-October through November.
Winter (December–February) still has spring temperatures, but rain is possible in both north and south.

WHAT'S ON

January *Festival de Musica de Canarias:* Santa Cruz.
February *Festival de la Virgen de la Candelaria:* Candelaria.
Carnival season (week before Ash Wednesday): major events in Santa Cruz and Puerto de la Cruz.
April *Holy Week:* processions prior to Easter and major events in La Laguna, Santa Cruz, Puerto de la Cruz, La Orotava.
May *Fiesta de la Cruz* in Puerto de la Cruz with floral crosses.
June *Feast of Corpus Christi:* flower carpets and processions on streets in La Orotava, and pilgrimage

processions in La Orotava and Los Realejos.
Fiesta de la Virgen del Carmen: in Puerto de la Cruz, Los Realejos and Santiago del Teide.
August *Festival de la Virgen de la Candelaria:* Candelaria.
Corazones de Tejina (last week): huge hearts of boughs, fruits and pastries are hoisted in the air to celebrate the harvest, La Laguna.
Romería: pilgrimage of San Roque, Garachico.
September *International Kite Festival:* Granadilla.
Fiesta de Nuestra Señora del Carmen (first week): Los Cristianos.

Fiestas (mid-month) in La Laguna, Granadilla, Tegueste, Valle de Guerra and San Miguel de Abona.
October *Fiesta de Santa Ursula de la Encarnación* (second week): Adeje.
November *Fiesta de San Andrés* (last week): Puerto de la Cruz. Celebration of the new wine. The night before is the *Arrastre los Cacharros,* when children drag metal pots through the streets.
Icod de los Viños: Greased sledges race down vertical streets; tasting of the new wine.
December *Christmas Day*: Tenerife Symphony Orchestra open-air concert, Santa Cruz.

Useful Websites

www.tenerifeisland.com
English site with excellent information on island transport, with relevant links. Airlines serving the islands are listed helpfully by country of flight origin. Other aspects of living and playing on Tenerife are covered, including detailed descriptions of beaches.

www.secret-tenerife.com
Local news and events, with perhaps the most complete listings available anywhere of everything from local festivals to shows and concerts. Along with the dates and times, this site includes historic and cultural details about local festivals that tourism brochures don't even mention.

www.spainexpat.com
Info—cultural, practical and legal—for those who make the Canary Islands their full-time or seasonal home, or are considering doing so. Although it covers the whole of Spain, the site helps demystify much of the red tape anyone living in the islands is likely to encounter.

www.webtenerifeuk.co.uk
This is the site of the Tenerife Tourism Corporation and full of helpful information about the island. Read about particular types of holidays and the best places for children.

www.spain.info
The Tourist Office of Spain's official website offers the most authoritative information on the island, with town-by-town descriptions that include tourist offices, museums, cuisine, places to eat, cultural events, beaches and much more.

www.alpharooms.com
User-friendly lodgings site with good prices and thorough descriptions of hotels and apartments to help you choose.

Getting There

ENTRY REQUIREMENTS

Visitors from EU countries, the USA and Canada need only a passport to enter the Canary Islands, unless they plan to stay longer than 90 days, in which case a residence permit or special visa is required. For up-to-date information visit www.britishembassy.gov.uk or http://travel.state.gov. Be sure to carry your passport with you when driving a car.

CUSTOMS

For customs purposes the Canary Islands are not members of the EU. The duty-free allowance for goods taken in or out (applicable to persons 17 and over) include: 2 litres of wine; 1 litre of spirits; 200 cigarettes (or 100 cigarillos or 50 cigars or 250g tobacco); 50ml perfume or 250ml toilet water; €175 worth of gifts per person.

AIRPORTS

Direct flights on more than 100 airlines from all over Europe arrive at Aeropuerto Tenerife Sur-Reina Sofía, one of the busiest in all Spain. Los Rodeos-Tenerife Norte handles most of the flights from mainland Spain, as well as inter-island flights.

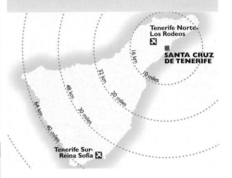

FROM TENERIFE SUR-REINA SOFÍA

Most international flights, including charters, arrive at Aeropuerto Tenerife Sur-Reina Sofía (www.aena.es ☎ 902 40 47 04 or 922 75 90 00). Only 18km (11 miles) from Los Cristianos, it is close to all the southern resorts, and reached by the TF1 motorway. It is 63km (39 miles) from Santa Cruz. The airport is open 24 hours a day.

TITSA (Transportes Interurbanos de Tenerife SA) buses, called *guaguas* (www.titsa.com, ☎ 922 53 13 00), numbers 111 and 487, connect to Los Cristianos; numbers 111 and 341 to Santa Cruz. Taxis are a better option to the nearby smaller resorts, which can only be reached via bus with an intricate series of connections. Expect to have to wait for a taxi after any large international arrival; be sure to agree on a rate in advance or insist on the metre rate, since they vary wildly.

Most package tours include airport transfer; watch for the signs as you enter the arrivals area. (If arriving on a charter, be sure to ask if you need to reconfirm the homeward-bound flight 72 hours before departure.)

FROM TENERIFE NORTE-LOS RODEOS

Tenerife Norte-Los Rodeos (www.aena.es ☎ 922 63 59 98) handles most of the flights arriving from mainland Spain, as well as inter-island flights. It is near La Laguna, 10km (6 miles) to the west of Santa Cruz and 26km (16 miles) northeast of Puerto de la Cruz via the TF5 motorway. It is 80km (50 miles) from Los Cristianos.

TITSA buses (www.titsa.com, ☎ 922 53 13 00), numbers 102 and 340 connect the airport to Puerto de la Cruz; numbers 102, 107 and 108 will take you to Santa Cruz. From Santa Cruz's central bus station a transfer to number 111 or 341 will take you to Los Cristianos. A taxi to Santa Cruz will cost about €25, depending on traffic.

ARRIVING BY BOAT

Acciona Trasmediterranea (www.trasmediter-ranea.es, ☎ 902 45 46 45) ferries sail from Cádiz, near Seville in mainland Spain, to Santa Cruz from mid-January through to the end of September, leaving at midnight on Tuesday and arriving at 8am Thursday. The return voyage leaves at 2pm Thursday and arrives 10am Saturday. The rough crossing and high rates, however, make air travel a much more attractive option unless you actually need to get a car to the island. Acciona also connects Santa Cruz to Las Palmas on Gran Canaria, but Binter airline (www.bintercanarias.com ☎ 902 39 13 92) does it faster.

TO LA GOMERA

Although Binter (www.bintercanarias.com ☎ 902 39 13 92) operates flights to La Gomera, the frequent boats from Los Cristianos to San Sebastián run by Naviera Armas (www.navieraarmas.com ☎ 902 45 65 00) and Fred Olsen Express (www.fredolsen.es ☎ 902 10 01 07) are both less expensive and much more convenient than arriving at the airport, which is high on mountainside above Playa de Santiago.

NEED TO KNOW GETTING THERE

INSURANCE

Although travellers from EU countries can receive emergency medical care at public facilities by presenting their European health card (EHIC) (known in Spain as a *Tarjeta Sanitaria Europea*), it is advisable for all visitors to carry health and travel insurance for the duration of their trip. The EHIC is not good for non-emergencies, at private clinics (often the preferable option here) or for dental emergencies. Nor will it cover the cost of medical evacuation home.

CONSULATES

British Consulate ✉ Plaza Weyler 8–1, Santa Cruz ☎ 922 28 68 63 ◎ Mon–Fri 8.30–1.30, shorter hours Jul–Aug

Consulate of Ireland ✉ Calle Castillo 8, Santa Cruz ☎ 922 24 56 71

US Consulate ✉ Calle Martinez de Escobar 3, Las Palmas, Gran Canaria ☎ 928 27 12 59

Getting Around

TOURIST OFFICES

Airport North ☎ 922 82 50 46 🕐 Daily 9–5

Airport South ☎ 922 39 20 37 🕐 Mon–Fri 9–9 (Jul–Sep 9–7), Sat–Sun 9–5

La Orotava ✉ Calle Calvario ☎ 922 32 30 41 🕐 Mon–Fri 8.30–6

Playa de las Américas ✉ Avenida Rafael Puig 19 ☎ 922 79 76 68 🕐 Mon–Fri 9–9, Sat 9–3.30

Puerto de la Cruz ✉ Plaza de Europa ☎ 922 38 60 00 🕐 Mon–Fri 9–8 (Jul–Sep 9–7), Sat 9–1 (Jul–Sep 9–12)

Santa Cruz ✉ Cabildo Insular, Plaza España ☎ 922 23 95 92 🕐 Mon–Fri 8–6 (Jul–Sep 8–5), Sat 9–1 (Jul–Sep 9–12)

San Sebastián, La Gomera ✉ Calle Real 4 ☎ 922 14 15 21 🕐 Mon–Sat 9–1.30, 3.30–6, Sun 10–1

Tenerife's bus system covers the entire island, but schedules are designed for the convenience of local commuters, not visitors wanting to go sightseeing. Hiring a car is the best way to see the island.

BUSES AND TRAMS
● TITSA (www.titsa.com ☎ 922 53 13 00) is the island bus company, and its *guaguas* (pronounced 'wah-wahs') reach nearly all towns.
● Check weekend schedules carefully, since service is limited or stops entirely.
● You can download a copy of the most current timetable or search for the most direct route between places on their website. A route map with timetable is also available at larger tourist offices.
● The tram system, Tranvia, runs every five minutes from the main bus station near the Parque Marítimo César Manrique in Santa Cruz to La Trinidad in La Laguna.
● The bus service on La Gomera is patchy and not very useful to visitors.

TICKETS
● Buy your ticket on the bus, telling the driver your destination.
● Rates are based on distances. If you plan to use the bus a lot, invest in a Bono-Vía, providing discounted rates for both the bus and tram. Buy one at bus stations or newsagents. Show it for discounted admission at government-run museums.

TAXIS
● For those without cars, taxis provide the best means of getting from bus stations to resorts for arrivals and departures with luggage.
● Taxis are available at the airports and at central points in larger towns (at Plaza del Charco in Puerto Cruz, for example). Your hotel can call one for you or you can ring Radio Taxi ☎ 922 64 11 12.
● Insist that the meter be running or agree on the rate for longer trips in advance.

HIRING A CAR

● Offices for the major car hire companies are at the airports and in all resort towns, and except at the busiest seasons it is usually possible to hire a car.

● Booking in advance assures the car of your choice and locks in a rate.

● If you do not see the firm you have reserved with at the airport, ask at one of the windows, since they often have local representatives, such as Cicar, the island's major car rental firm.

● It is important to book a car a day ahead for La Gomera so it will await you at the ferry or airport.

DRIVING

● Driving is on the right, a challenge for those from left-driving countries. Be especially cautious when entering roundabouts and coming onto main roads from smaller ones.

● Mountain roads are often steep and narrow, although they are usually in good repair. In some places roads narrow to a single lane and approaching cars must pull into a layby to pass. Where single-lane bridges cross the ends of *barrancos*, signs advise which driver has the right of way.

● Most signage is quite good and exits from motorways are well marked.

● Rental car contracts prohibit driving on unpaved roads except in a four-wheel-drive car.

● There are hefty on-the-spot fines for not wearing seatbelts, failing to stop at a Stop sign or for overtaking in a forbidden zone, and random breath tests are also carried out.

BICYCLES

● Although roads along the coast tend to be relatively level, the entire inland of the island rises to steep mountains, so roads provide a serious workout for cyclists.

● Do not expect drivers to make accommodation for cyclists, and beware that verges often have drainage ditches and very sharp drop-offs at the edge of the metalled surface.

VISITORS WITH A DISABILITY

Facilities for those with limited mobility are improving, with ramps, lifts and other accommodations becoming more common. Newer hotels will usually have specially equipped rooms available. Le Ro (☎ 922 75 02 89; www.Lero.net) provides airport transfers with an adaptive minibus and can deliver wheelchairs and other equipment to hotels or apartments. Beaches, especially at Los Cristianos, have well-marked wheelchair access ramps and boardwalks.

ORGANIZED SIGHTSEEING

Atlantico Excursiones (☎ 922 71 66 45; www.atlanticoexcursiones.com) operates a full schedule of island tours, covering the highlights, including Teide National Park, La Orotava, Icod, Garachico, Candalaria and even a shopping excursion to Santa Cruz. Colour Tours (☎ 922 75 08 11) gets a bit closer to the land with tours of the mountainous inland of both Tenerife and La Gomera in four-wheel-drive vehicles.

NEED TO KNOW GETTING AROUND

Essential Facts

MONEY

The official currency in the Canary Islands is the euro (€). Banknotes come in denominations of €5, €10, €20, €50, €100, €200 and €500 and 1, 2, 5, 10, 20, 50 cent and €1 and €2 euro coins.

5 euros

10 euros

50 euros

100 euros

ELECTRICITY

● The current throughout the islands is 220 volts AC, and sockets take the circular two-pin continental-style plug.

ETIQUETTE

● Canarians are accustomed to visitors and are generally not fussy about formalities.
● Other diners will often greet anyone entering a restaurant, and it's courteous to return the greeting or at least smile and nod.

EMERGENCY NUMBERS

Emergency and security services on the islands are integrated.
● For all emergencies ☎ 112
● Ambulance ☎ 061
● Policía Nacional (National Police) ☎ 091
● Guardia Civil (Civil Guard) ☎ 062
● Guardia Civil de Tráfico (traffic police) ☎ 922 66 24 41

LOST PROPERTY

● At the airport: North Airport ☎ 922 63 58 55, South Airport ☎ 922 75 93 91
● Elsewhere: Report stolen or lost property to the Local Police or to the Guardia Civil (see emergency numbers above). Get a copy of the report for your insurance claim.

MAIL

● Post offices, *correos*, ◉ Mon–Fri 9–2, Sat 9–1. Santa Cruz ☎ 922 53 36 29, Puerto de la Cruz ☎ 922 38 58 05, Los Cristianos ☎ 922 79 10 56
● Look for yellow post boxes and use the '*extranjeros*' slot for mail back home.
● Stamps are *sellos* and can also be bought at tobacconists and at stores that sell postcards.

MEDICAL TREATMENT

● Adeje: USP Hospital Costa Adeje ☎ 922 75 26 26
● Puerto de la Cruz: Clínica y Centros Médicos Vida ☎ 902 31 31 81

Hospital Bellevue ☎ 922 38 35 51
Hospital Tamaragua ☎ 922 38 05 12
● Santa Cruz: Hospital Nuestra Señora de
Candelaria ☎ 922 60 20 00
● La Laguna: Hospital Universitario de Canarias
☎ 922 67 80 00
Hospital Rambla ☎ 922 29 16 00
Arona: Hospital Sur ☎ 922 75 00 22

MONEY MATTERS
● There is no limit to the amount of money
you may bring onto the islands, but you are not
allowed to take out more than €3,000.
● ATM cash dispensers are common.
● Many small restaurants and shops don't take
credit cards.

OPENING TIMES
● Banks: Mon–Fri 8.30–2.30, also Sep–Apr Sat
8.30–12.30.
● Shops: Generally 9–2, 5–8 except in shopping malls, where shops are open 9.30am–
10pm.

SENSIBLE PRECAUTIONS
● Street crime is quite rare in Tenerife and La
Gomera, but visitors should not be complacent.
Uniformed police are always present in tourist
areas. The greatest risk is assault or theft by
another tourist.
● Lock doors and windows before going out.
Put all valuables in the boot of your car.
● Do not leave possessions unattended on the
beach.
● Fire is a risk in hotels—locate the nearest fire
exit to your room and ensure it is not blocked
or locked.

TELEPHONES
● With the proliferation of mobile phones,
public phones are becoming less common, but
if you need to make a call, most bars and cafés
will let you use the phone for a minimal charge.
● To call outside of Spain, dial 01 before the
country code, for example 0144 to call the UK.

NATIONAL HOLIDAYS
● 1 January: New Year's Day
● 6 January: Epiphany
● 1 May: Labour Day
● 15 August: Assumptión
● 12 October: Columbus Day
● 1 November: All Saints'
Day
● 6 December: Constitution
Day
● 8 December: Immaculate
Conception
● 25 December: Christmas
Day
● Moveable feasts are
Maundy Thursday and Good
Friday.

PLACES OF WORSHIP
English speaking services:
● Puerto de la Cruz:
Anglican Church ✉ Parque
Taoro 🕘 Sun 9.30, 11;
Nuestra Señora de la Peña
✉ Plaza Iglesia 🕘 Sun
10; Evangelical Church
✉ Careterra Taoro 🕘 Sun
11.30, Wed 4.30, 5pm.
● Adeje: Anglican Church
of the Canarian People
🕘 Sun 10.
● Arona: Guadalupe Church
🕘 Sat 6pm, Sun 10am.
● Los Cristianos: La Virgen
del Carmen 🕘 Daily 5.30,
Sun and Wed noon.

Language

Spanish is spoken in the Canary Islands. People working in the tourist industry generally know some English, but if you venture off the beaten track, including into some bars and restaurants in Santa Cruz, it's helpful to know some basic Spanish. Pronunciation guide: *b* almost like *v*; *c* before *e* or *i* sounds like *th* otherwise like *k*; *d* can be like English *d* or softer *th*; *g* before *e* or *i* is a guttural *h*, otherwise *g*; *h* always silent; *j* guttural *h*; *ll* like *lli* in million; *ñ* like *ni* in onion; *qu* like *k*; *v* like *b*; *z* like *th*.

COURTESIES

good morning	*buenos días*
good afternoon/evening	*buenas tardes*
good night	*buenas noches*
hello (informal)	*hola*
goodbye (informal)	*hasta luego/hasta pronto*
hello (answering phone)	*¿Diga?*
goodbye	*adios*
please	*por favor*
thank you	*gracias*
you're welcome	*de nada*
how are you? (formal)	*¿Como está?*
how are you? (informal)	*¿Que tal?*
I'm fine	*estoy bien*
I'm sorry	*lo siento*
excuse me (in a bar)	*oiga*
excuse me (in a crowd)	*perdón*

USEFUL WORDS

I don't know	*No lo sé*
I don't think so	*Creo que no*
I think so	*Creo que sí*
It doesn't matter	*No importa*
Where?	*¿Dónde?*
When?	*¿Cuándo?*
Why?	*¿Por qué?*
What?	*¿Que?*
Who?	*¿Quién?*
How?	*¿Cómo?*
How much/many?	*¿Cuánto/cuántos?*
Is/are there?	*¿Hay?*
ticket	*entrada*

DAYS

Monday	*lunes*
Tuesday	*martes*
Wednsday	*miércoles*
Thursday	*jueves*
Friday	*viernes*
Saturday	*sábado*
Sunday	*domingo*
today	*hoy*
yesterday	*ayer*
tomorrow	*mañana*

NUMBERS

1	*uno*
2	*dos*
3	*tres*
4	*cuatro*
5	*cinco*
6	*seis*
7	*siete*
8	*ocho*
9	*nueve*
10	*diez*
11	*once*
12	*doce*
13	*trece*
14	*catorce*
15	*quince*
16	*dieciséis*
17	*diecisiete*
18	*dieciocho*
19	*diecinueve*
20	*veinte*

BASIC VOCABULARY

yes/no	*sí/no*
I don't understand	*no entiendo*
I don't speak Spanish	*no hablo español*
left/right	*izquierda/derecha*
entrance/exit	*entrada/salida*
open/closed	*abierto/cerrado*
good/bad	*bueno/mal*
big/small	*grande/pequeño*
with/without	*con/sin*
more/less	*más/menos*
hot/cold	*caliente/frío*
early/late	*temprano/tarde*
here/there	*aquí/alli*
today/tomorrow	*hoy/mañana*
yesterday	*ayer*
how much is it?	*¿cuanto es?*
where is the…?	*¿dónde está…?*
do you have…?	*¿tiene…?*
I'd like…	*me gustaría*
my name is…	*me llamo…*

FOOD

apple	*manzana*
banana	*plátano*
beans	*habas*
chicken	*pollo*
clams	*almejas*
duck	*pato*
fish	*pescado*
fruit	*fruta*
lamb	*cordero*
lettuce	*lechuga*
lobster	*langosta*
meat	*carne*
melon	*melón*
orange	*naranja*
pork	*cerdo*
seafood	*marsicos*
shrimps	*gambas*
squid	*calamare*
tomato	*tomate*
tuna	*atún*
turkey	*pavo*

EATING OUT

smoking allowed	*se permite fumar*
no smoking	*se prohibe fumar*
menu	*la carta*
fork	*tenedor*
knife	*cuchillo*
spoon	*cuchara*
napkin	*servilleta*
glass of wine	*copa*
glass of beer	*caña*
water (mineral)	*agua (mineral)*
still/sparkling	*sin gas/con gas*
coffee (with milk)	*café (con leche)*
May I have the bill?	*La cuenta, por favor*
Do you take credit cards?	*¿Aceptan tarjetas de crédito?*
cakes	*pasteles*
small snacks	*pinchos*
sandwiches	*bocadillos*
set dishes	*platos combinados*

SHOPPING

ATM/cash machine	*cajero*
I want to buy…	*quiero comprar…*
I'm just looking	*sólo estoy mirando*
belt	*cinturón*
blouse	*blusa*
dress	*vestido*
shirt	*camisa*
shoes	*zapatas*
skirt	*falda*
tie	*corbata*
small	*pequeño*
medium	*mediano*
large	*grande*
cotton	*algodón*
silk	*seda*
wool	*lana*

NEED TO KNOW LANGUAGE

Timeline

THE FIRST ISLANDERS

Guanches, the first settlers, lived Stone Age lives, raising some crops and herding goats. They were accomplished potters and roasted and ground grains for food, using handmade mills. That grain product, *gofio,* is still a staple on the island. While popular history relates that the Guanches were exterminated, local author Jose Luis Concepción, in *The Guanches, Survivors and their Descendants,* argues convincingly that most survived periods of slavery and that their descendants are today's islanders.

From left: Iglesia de la Asunción, San Sebastián, La Gomera; statue of Guanche chief, Candelaria; Torre del Condo, San Sebastián; Bananera El Guanche; old ships in Los Cristianos harbour; El Tigre, the cannon that cost Admiral Nelson his arm, in the Museo Militar, Santa Cruz

1st century BC First settlers, probably Berber and Cro-Magnon from the Mediterranean, settle the islands. Later known as Guanches, they remain a Stone Age people into the 15th century.

1st century AD Romans visit islands, Pliny the Elder and Ptolemy note their existence.

1339–42 Spanish explorers learn of the Canary Islands and begin searching for them.

1404–6 Juan de Bethencourt seeks to conquer Tenerife but fails and returns to France.

1445 Conquest of La Gomera begins and San Sebastián is settled.

1478–88 Ferdinand and Isabella of Castile order the conquest of the islands.

1492 Christopher Columbus stops at La Gomera to re-provision before sailing off and discovering the Americas.

1494–6 Fernández de Lugo begins the conquest of Tenerife, culminating in the Battle of Acentejo on Christmas Day 1495.

1797 In 1796 Spain had allied itself with Revolutionary France so is at war with Britain; Admiral Horatio Nelson attacks Santa Cruz, but is repulsed and loses his arm in the battle.

1830s Tenerife's wine industry collapses due to phylloxera infestations—wine had been the island's major export. Cochineal industry forms but fails by mid-century.

1852 Queen Isabella declares Santa Cruz de Tenerife a free-trade zone.

1880s Banana industry established, serving the European market.

1936 The Spanish Republic exiles General Francisco Franco to the Canary Islands as Military Governor. On 17 July he announces the beginning of the Spanish Civil War.

1982 Under the new post-Franco constitution, the Canary Islands become an autonomous region.

1986 Garajonay National Park, La Gomera, becomes a UNESCO World Heritage Site.

1999 La Laguna recognised as a UNESCO World Heritage Site.

2003 Santiago Calatrava's Auditorio opens in Santa Cruz.

2008 President of the Tenerife Cabildo (council) announces 10-year plan to create train service from Santa Cruz to Los Cristianos. Forest fires burn more than 1,700 acres (6,880ha) on La Gomera and threaten Garajonay National Park.

COLUMBUS ISLAND

When Columbus sailed for India in 1492 he stopped in La Gomera for water and provisions. He stayed longer than necessary, some say because of local beauty Beatriz de Bobadilla. He continued to make visits to the island until he learned of her marriage. A change of the island's name was once suggested to honour his stays here.

ADMIRAL'S FOLLY

After several attempts, Admiral Horatio Nelson attacked Santa Cruz on 25 July 1797 with 900 soldiers in an attempt to capture a ship recently arrived loaded with riches from the Caribbean. During the battle the admiral's arm was struck by a shell and had to be amputated. After fierce fighting in the streets against local militia, the British surrendered and were allowed to depart on promising to attack the islands no more.

Index

INDEX

TWINPACK
Tenerife

WRITTEN BY Barbara Radcliffe Rogers and Stillman Rogers
VERIFIED BY Penny Phenix and Hilary Weston
COVER DESIGN AND DESIGN WORK Jacqueline Bailey
INDEXER Marie Lorimer
IMAGE RETOUCHING AND REPRO Sarah Montgomery, Michael Moody and James Tims
PROJECT EDITOR Stephanie Smith
SERIES EDITOR Cathy Harrison

© **AA MEDIA LIMITED 2010**
Reprinted December 2010

Colour separation by AA Digital Department
Printed and bound by Leo Paper Products, China

A CIP catalogue record for this book is available from the British Library.

ISBN 978-0-7495-6155-0

Published by AA Publishing, a trading name of AA Media Limited, whose registered office is Fanum House, Basing View, Basingstoke, Hampshire RG21 4EA. Registered number 06112600.

Front cover image: AA/C Jones
Back cover images: (i) AA/C Sawyer; (ii) AA/C Sawyer; (iii) AA/J Tims; (iv) AA/C Jones

A04619
Maps in this title produced from mapping © MAIRDUMONT / Falk Verlag 2011

The Automobile Association would like to thank the following photographers, companies and picture libraries for their assistance in the preparation of this book.

Abbreviations for the pictures credits are as follows – (t) top; (b) bottom; (c) centre; (l) left; (r) right; (AA) AA World Travel Library.

1 AA/C Sawyer; 2–18 top panel AA/C Jones; 4 AA/C Jones; 5 AA/C Sawyer; 6tl AA/J Tims; 6tc AA/C Jones; 6tr AA/C Sawyer; 6bl AA/J Tims; 6br Brand X Pics; 7tl AA/J Tims; 7tr AA/C Sawyer; 7bl AA/C Jones; 7bc AA/C Jones; 7br AA/C Sawyer; 10t AA/J Tims; 10c(i) AA/J Tims; 10c(ii) AA/C Jones; 10b AA/C Jones; 11t(i) AA/C Jones; 11t(ii) AA/J Tims; 11c(i) AA/C Jones; 11c(ii) AA/C Jones; 11b AA/C Jones; 12t AA/C Sawyer; 12c(i) AA/R Moore; 12c(ii) AA/C Sawyer; 12b AA/C Sawyer; 13t(i) AA/C Sawyer; 13t(ii) AA/C Sawyer; 13c(i) AA/C Sawyer; 13c(ii) AA/C Sawyer; 13b Royalty Free Photodisc; 14t AA/J Tims; 14c(i) AA/M Jourdan; 14c(ii) AA/C Sawyer; 14b AA/M Jourdan; 15 AA/R Moore; 16t AA/R Moore; 16c Imagestate; 16b AA/C Sawyer; 17t Digitalvision; 17c AA/J Tims; 17b Hotel Bahia Gran Duque; 18t AA/C Jones; 18c(i) AA/C Jones; 18c(ii) AA/C Jones; 18b AA/R Moore; 19t AA/C Jones; 19c(i) AA/J Tims; 19c(ii) AA/C Jones; 19b AA/C Jones; 20/21 AA/R Moore; 24l AA/C Sawyer; 24r AA/C Sawyer; 25l AA/C Sawyer; 25c AA/C Sawyer; 25r AA/R Moore; 26 AA/C Jones; 26/27 AA/C Jones; 27 AA/R Moore; 28l AA/C Jones; 28r AA/C Jones; 29 AA/C Sawyer; 30l AA/C Jones; 30c AA/C Jones; 30r AA/C Jones; 31l AA/C Jones; 31r AA/C Jones; 32 AA/J Tims; 33t AA/C Jones; 33bl AA/C Jones; 33br AA/C Jones; 34t Courtesy of Museo de la Naturaleza y el Hombre de Tenerife; 34bl AA/R Moore; 34br Courtesy of Museo de la Naturaleza y el Hombre de Tenerife; 35l AA/C Jones; 35r AA/C Jones; 36 Chris Howes/Wild Places Photography/Alamy; 37 AA/J Tims; 38l AA/J Tims; 38/39 AA/C Jones; 39r AA/J Tims; 40–42 top panel AA/J Tims; 40l AA/R Moore; 40r AA/J Tims; 41l AA/J Tims; 41r AA/C Jones; 42l AA/C Jones; 42r AA/C Sawyer; 43 AA/C Jones; 44 AA/C Jones; 45 AA/R Moore; 46 AA/C Jones; 47–48 AA/C Sawyer; 49 AA/C Jones; 52l AA/C Sawyer; 52r AA/R Moore; 53l AA/J Tims; 53r AA/J Tims; 54l AA/C Jones; 54br AA/J Tims; 54/55 AA/C Sawyer; 55bl AA/C Jones; 55br AA/C Jones; 56t AA/C Sawyer; 56bl AA/C Jones; 56br AA/C Jones; 57tl AA/C Jones; 57bl AA/C Jones; 57r AA/C Jones; 58l AA/C Sawyer; 58r AA/C Sawyer; 59l AA/C Sawyer; 59r AA/C Jones; 60l Bernard Loison www.mytho-fleurs.com; 60r Bernard Loison www.mytho-fleurs.com; 61 Bernard Loison www.mytho-fleurs.com; 62t AA/C Sawyer; 62b AA/C Sawyer; 62/63 AA/C Sawyer; 63r AA/C Sawyer; 64l AA/R Moore; 64tr AA/J Tims; 64br AA/C Sawyer; 65tl AA/R Moore; 65bl AA/C Jones; 65r AA/C Jones; 66l AA/C Jones; 66tr AA/C Jones; 66br AA/C Jones; 67t AA/C Jones; 67bl AA/J Tims; 67br AA/C Jones; 68–70 top panel AA/C Sawyer; 68 AA/C Jones; 69l AA/C Sawyer; 69r AA/C Jones; 70l AA/C Jones; 70r AA/R Moore; 71 AA/C Sawyer; 72 AA/R Moore; 73 AA/C Jones; 74 AA/C Jones; 75 AA/C Jones; 76l AA/C Sawyer; 76tr AA/C Jones; 76br AA/C Jones; 77t AA/R Moore; 77bl AA/J Tims; 77br AA/C Jones; 80t AA/C Jones; 80b AA/R Moore; 80/81 AA/C Jones; 82–84 top panel AA/C Jones; 82l AA/C Jones; 82r AA/J Tims; 83l AA/R Moore; 83r AA/C Jones; 84l AA/R Moore; 84r AA/C Sawyer; 85 AA/J Tims; 86 AA/J Tims; 87 Imagebroke/Alamy; 88 AA/R Moore; 89 AA/C Jones; 90 AA/C Sawyer; 91 AA/C Sawyer; 94 AA/C Jones; 94/95 AA/C Sawyer; 95 AA/C Jones ; 96l AA/C Jones; 96tr AA/C Jones; 9br AA/C Sawyer; 97t AA/C Jones; 97bl AA/C Jones; 97br AA/C Sawyer; 98l AA/C Jones; 98tr AA/C Sawyer; 98br AA/C Jones; 99 AA/C Jones; 100–101 top panel AA/C Jones; 100l Courtesy of La Gomera Tourist Board; 100r AA/C Jones; 101l AA/C Jones; 101r AA/C Sawyer; 102 AA/C Jones; 103 AA/C Jones; 104 AA/C Jones; 105t AA/R Moore; 105b AA/C Jones; 106 AA/C Jones; 107 AA/R Moore; 108–112 top panel AA/C Sawyer; 108t AA/R Moore; 108c(i) AA/C Sawyer; 108(ii) AA/M Chaplow; 108b AA/J Tims; 113 AA/C Jones; 114–125 top panel AA/J Tims; 120 MRI Bankers' Guide to Foreign Currency, Houston, USA; 124l AA/C Sawyer; 124c AA/C Sawyer; 124r AA/C Sawyer; 125l AA/C Sawyer; 125c AA/C Jones; 125r AA/R Moore.

Every effort has been made to trace the copyright holders, and we apologise in advance for any accidental errors. We would be happy to apply any corrections in the following edition of this publication.